House of the Mother

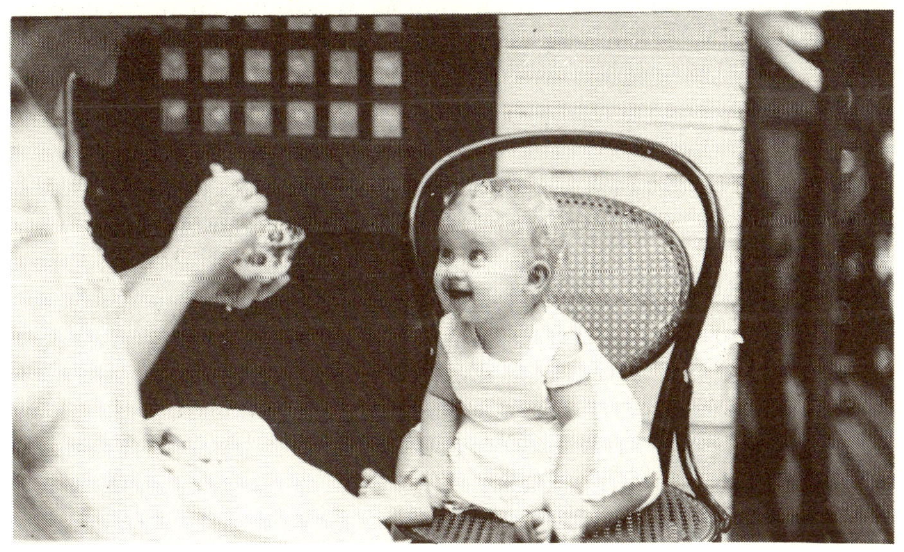

Susan Bright

Austin Book Award, 1994

Plain View Press
P. O. 33311
Austin, TX 78764
512-441-2452

Photo by James Dwight Safford

ISBN: 0-911-51-79-1
Library of Congress Number: 94-68260

Short quotations from the work of women writers in the following pages were taken from two books: **Norton Anthology of Literature by Women**, Sandra M. Gilbert and Susan Bugar, editors, W.W. Norton, 1985; and **Women Poets from Antiquity to Now**, Aliki and Willis Barnstone, editors, Shocken Books, 1980.

Acknowledgements

"Do Not Forget in Peace Times" was published in **Borderlands,** Vol. I, No. 2, 1993; **"Enheduenna Wrote on Stone"** was published in **Women's Way, 1991** and broadcast of **W.I.N.G.S**, an international radio series; *"Creek"* was published in the **Houston Poetry Festival Anthology,** 1992 and in **Tirades and Evidence of Grace**, 1992 (Plain View Press); *"Our Lady of Guadalupe"* was published in the **Bilingual Review,** Vol XIII, No. 3, 1986 ; *"Greenwood Street"* was published in **Far Side of the Word**, 1987 (Plain View Press); *"Iris"* was published in **"Atomic Basket,"** 1985 (InBetween Books). Premier readings of many of these poems were presented on John Aielli's *Eklektos* program, public radio station (KUT), Austin, TX.

Thanks

Thanks to Glee Ingram for wise help editing and sequencing; to Megan Bright, Betty Sue Flowers, Jane Richardson and Sheetal Nasta for proofreading and editing ideas; to Sarah Bolz for artistic help, to Butch Hancock for showing me how to look at photographs; to Mike Morgan for printing expertise; to Roe Fleenor for camera work; to John C. Andrews and Daryl Bright Andrews for time and space in which to work, to Helen Bright Bryant for inspiration, to Anne Bright for the whole shebang, to a thousand grandmothers, to a generation willing to claim the healing power of the mother.

Support for this book was granted in part by the City of Austin Arts Commission and Texas Circuit through the Austin Book Award Program.

About the Cover

Cover photo of Maude Smith Safford was taken when she was in high school in Deposit, New York. The hand-tinted panoramas were taken by James Dwight Safford in China sometime between 1911 and 1918. The text on the back cover is from a letter from George May Cure Bright to my father. Part of the letter is included in the text on page 16. She called the fancy slashes *"accents"* and used them to create flourish.

Contents

Introductory note to family and friends who find themselves misnamed, misquoted, misunderstood—

I was amused to read in two reviews of my last book that I write about my experience as a single parent. Nothing could be further from the truth. My son has a full time father, as I had. Lots of children don't. I write about some of those children.

I write about everything I can fit into my head and I scramble facts the way Mark Twain did when he moved a county from one side of the Mississippi River to the other, *"for the sake of literature."*

I'm not trying to create a family history, or an autobiography. Nor am I careless of the truth. I use what I call an *Experimental I*, much the same way empathy lets us *live* things at the movies we don't have to exactly experience.

I am using ethnographic material to look at the heart of the family, at the house of the Mother. I've been trying to understand how the mothers and grandmothers, fathers and grandfathers, could have allowed the horrible momentum of so violent a century as we have just experienced.

I think it is because women have had not had the power to keep their sons out of the military, out of jail. But I think it is deeper than that because we've seen women in power be as idiotic as men ever thought of being. Even women have lost the healing power of the mother. I've been looking for it.

When I was at Stanford, Ivor Winters was basking in *New Criticism* and the *Bay Area Renaissance*. He said a poem should be understood as an independent work of art. He said the life of the poet had nothing to do with *his* work.

I find the line between life and art more like a dance, a revolving door. I am the poems I write, and vice versa—just as real, or unreal are we both from/to each other as sunlight on water—and just as mercurial.

SB
11/15/94

Many of these photographs were taken by James Dwight Safford (1879-1920), my mother's father. He worked for the international YWCA from 1900-1920, and was stationed in Panama, Washington State and then in Manila. Grandmother Safford, when I knew her, was plain-faced and subdued, but the Maude in the photographs was a different person entirely. She was beautiful and alive, a woman in love, a radiant new mother. Mother was six and her brother was four when everything changed. Dwight died of encephalitis, leaving my grandmother with no pension and two small children to raise. Encephalitis degenerates to madness. There was no money.

The world was at war. The optimism of the early years of the century flipped. Maude sent Dwight to a sanitarium in Philadelphia where he died. What we know of him comes from photographs made of shadow, contrast and passion. He saw innocence and light at the beginning of the twentieth century, but he also saw the unraveling.

George May Cure Bright was the only child of five to survive childhood on the farm at Four Corners, and she loved the place. Her grandparents bought it in the early 1800's and she intended that it not be lost. Here she is with my father, age one and Helen, age six. But everyone loses land, possibly because it can't be owned.

Four Corners

"Where is the town?"
I asked Mother.
"There isn't any,"
she told me,
"It's just four corners."

Mother Ape

Bow legs
spun
through time,
she
chipped flint
for ten thousand
years,
carved tools,
loped
huffing, grunting
farting, squealing
season to season,
squatted in birth,
picked nits
from wild tufts
of baby fur,
curled toothless
to a fetal
knot
and died.

She
painted cave walls
with berry juice—
and at the instant
that the painting
became more important
than the berries—
Mother Ape
invented ritual,
heard the sacred
names of *Water*
Sun, Moon,
talked to birds
and wind—
dreamed, and then
invented
us.

Photo by James Dwight Safford

Mother Politics

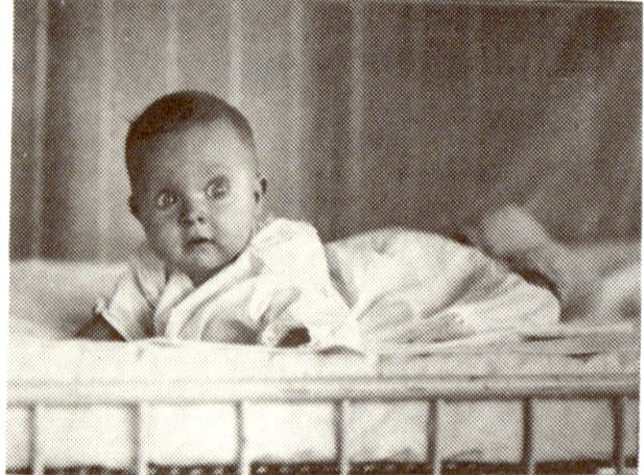

for a woman who told me
"I have three children to take care of.
I don't have time to register to vote."

How can you raise a sane child in a world full
of violence, where sex play can kill you,
where children carry guns to school in their lunch boxes,
where television is a god and everyone hates women?

How can you raise a sane child in a world
where a living species goes extinct every seven minutes,
where water is poisoned, where we use up in a decade
water reserves that took ten million years to fill up?

The book of the mother—
How to say it?

It is not enough to fill the refrigerator with milk.
Look how dairy cows jammed into small pens stand
on mounds of their own shit, while farmers inject them
with hormones and antibiotics.

How can we raise children whose immune systems work
when we feed them from birth the subtle poison
of milk in plastic bottles?
How to say it?

It is not enough to take the children to school or pay taxes.
An idiot has control of the schools, has created them
in its own image,
Mother, mother politics—
"It takes a whole village to raise a child."
(African Folk Saying)

Photo by James Dwight Safford

Ancestral House

There were storms outside the ancestral house. I've seen them for a thousand years, gathering on the horizon, great black swirling clouds that sprang out of the animal heart before there was a mind, before there were houses, before storms gathered, I have stood on the threshold listening for a language and heard none and wandered alone in the garden while the mother shrieked. I have watched great storms howl out of the womb of the mother, watched scraped blood storming, swirling at the house. I have been the shrieking mother. White streaks of lightning have cracked the galaxy *First Woman* threw out with hot ash at the beginning of the myth. I have been listening for a word. And there was no one I would listen to. Where is the song of the mother? Wrenched from pain, out of passion and spring rain, out of the waters of the universe, life force, force fields, rhythm, repetition—where is the song of the mother? Outside the ancestral house, the storms are still raging. Inside, an aging actress turns belly up and dreams. A woman dressed in hot iron lace hovers in the side yard. She is trying to kill me. There was a story—sometimes, when lightning was particularly intense, Grandmother could see a spiral of light spinning down the upstairs hallway. A small blond headed girl stands on the upstairs balcony, shouts to the canyons and they echo—echo the song of the child beginning, reaching for life, reaching out of the shriek of the mother, standing under the hovering blood storms. A large mastiff gnaws on the carved leg of a mahogany library table and mildew smolders in the basement. Pretenders have stolen the ancestral house and the wail of the mother seeps into infinite fractures in the canyon where waterfalls pitch deep into coal mountains, whole mountains on fire.

Photo by James Dwight Safford

Geography

Children live in a child's world, schools we create for them grow out of communities we create for ourselves. We hang a world map in the kitchen to keep track of the planet. **Kazakhstan** is the ninth largest country in the world, a vast plateau in central Asia, one of the countries that emerged from behind the Iron Curtain at the end of the twentieth century, the third best climate in the world. **Hong Kong** has a population density of 14,188 people per square mile. **Colombia** imports machinery, transportation equipment, food, and chemicals. *Chemicals?* Cocaine. Mountain villagers distill ancient medicine with bare hands and feet, like French wine. Columbia—three hundred thousand people dead between 1940 and 1960, *La Violencia*, a civic disorder. *Disorder?* Three hundred thousand people? In **Croatia,** ten thousand people were killed in a war between Muslims, Roman Catholics and Orthodox believers in 1991. Rape camps were set up on all sides of the conflict so that the men fought each other but everyone fought the women. The Croatian policy called *"ethnic cleansing"* explains mass graves full of Muslims and Serbs with bullet holes in their heads and backs. *Ethnic cleansing?* These are the hordes from the North, barbarians. W.W.I started when one of them assassinated an Austrian Prince, but there is no center to violence, it is everywhere. **Benin** is a small country in Africa where slave traders bartered with the Dahomey Kingdom on what became known as the Slave Coast in the seventeenth and eighteenth centuries. The per capita income is $381. **Ghana** exports cocoa, aluminum, petroleum, wood—and A.I.D.S. Everyone has it. **Nauru**, one of the world's smallest countries, is an island in the South Pacific Sea. The economy depends on mining and exporting phosphates. Eighty percent of Nauru has been destroyed. Now the people have to decide where to go. We put an atlas in the kitchen so we can study geography. But it is making us ill.

from *World Facts and Maps*, Rand McNally, 1993 Edition.

Photo by James Dwight Safford

Brigid

Time rolled over;   it was cold
Night rolled in;   it was dark.
Winter held;   and frost breath
froze the baby,   solid like stone
baby after baby,   turned to stone,
until *Sky* broke   and *Fire* fell
into the heart   of a maiden
weeping   frozen tears,
tears that   melted,
flowed   like water,
and *Fire*   held the dance
the life/force,   the dance,
and song   leaped out,
and pebbles   turned
to children   and more children
who gathered   stones
themselves   and then
built   walls
around   *Fire*
to keep   her alive.

George May Cure Bright,
age 16

And when   the maiden died
another maiden,   and another
protected   *Fire* light
which fell   from mother *Sky*,
protected *Fire*   which melted stone
and brought   the children
back   from death,
protected *Fire*   who melted ice
and filled   creek beds
with cold,   life,
green ferns,   protected *Fire*
who created   Spring.

So long,   these maidens
of the forest   protected *Fire*,
they learned   to self ignite.
Fire sparks   fell into words,
Fire sparks   fell into law,
to social order   held together
by the power   of the women
who caught   *Fire*
as she fell   from *Sky*
and then refused   to let her die.
Even now   you can see it
in their   eyes.

Grandmother had an interesting name. She was George because her father got tired of waiting for a boy.
May was for Spring. Cure means to heal. Bright comes from the name of the Goddess of Fire, Brigid.

Aurora

"The sky this morning was much like that in the famous painting of Aurora—save for the figures of Apollo and Aurora with her maidens and they were readily imagined. The landscape here abouts seemed a new country for a heavy mist had placed in mysterious places mirage-like lakes; only when I had opened the door on the front porch was I certain that our ancient house still stood in its accustomed place.

At the east end of the house which for a century has been in the family (if it still stands a century longer, hope it may remain ours, despite your now unsettled ideas concerning property) stand holly hocks of maroon, rose and lemon yellow, eight feet tall this year and planted when the house came into Grandfather's hands long, long, ago.

At the west end of the house grows still the rose that grandmother brought from her girlhood homestead in Clinton Township near Bethany. She had planted it at their first home with the peonies and other shrubs and after her tragic death, Grandfather transplanted them up here in memory of her for whom he had bought this place.

Yes, I was really at home even though the morning mist had seemed a sorcerer!

Now the mist is vanishing and everywhere dewdrops and the residue of the mist glisten like diamonds in the sun."

July 27, 1950
George May Cure Bright
(from a letter to son,
William E. Bright)

16

Landscape of Horror

Mary Wollstonecraft,
(1759-1797)
slept on the landing
outside her mother's
bedroom door to protect
her from Father, violent,
drunk, a bad farmer who
squandered her mother's
family fortune.

When there was no food
they sent her away, saying
she'll make a good
governess. She
founded a school. She
worked as a political
pamphleteer, in Paris,
a revolutionary pamphleteer. Heads rolled.

She wrote "*A Vindication of the Rights of Woman*," which was ignored
for three hundred years. Thomas Paine's, "*A Vindication of the Rights
of Man*," became a world classic.
They were published in the same year.

She said, "*It is time to effect a revolution in female manners—
time to restore to them their lost dignity—and make them,
as part of the human species, labour by reforming themselves,
to reform the world.*"

During the Reign of Terror her American husband left her with a baby
daughter, Fanny. He was a thief. He was unfaithful.
She jumped off Putney Bridge into the Thames River in despair.
It didn't kill her and she didn't stop working.

That year she published, "*A Historical and Moral View of the Origins and
Progress of the French Revolution.*"
She wrote to her husband begging him
to return. He didn't.

After that she met William Godwin, a philosopher.
They wrote together that men and women should be partners
in marriage. They believed women should be educated.
Most weren't.

She died of puerperal fever, an infected placenta ripped out
by physicians who didn't wash before surgery—
Midwives and their scrubbing had been banished.
Infection poisoned her milk.

They gave her wine for the pain
and brought puppies from the barn to suck her bad milk.
The baby was Mary Wollstonecraft Godwin Shelley.
She played in the graveyard.

Lonely child, she curled up alongside her dead mother's tombstone
to nap. A girl, she married Percy Bysshe Shelley, a poet, and one evening
she bet Lord Byron she could write a better horror
story than he could.

It came first in a dream—
a great monster generated by *"a pale student of unhallowed arts
who employed a powerful engine to awaken the hideous phantasm
of a man."*

Frankenstein, a child killing idiot born of a landscape of horror—
For three hundred years scholars disregarded Mary Wollstonecraft's work
saying she was, *"an hysterical woman."*

Some Women I Know

One has recently
returned
from war in the
Middle East.
Six are victims of
child abuse.
Seven have been raped.
Two have had
life threats leveled
at them
for political work.
One has A.I.D.S.
One is schizophrenic.
One suffers
chronic depression.
One's partner
was killed
in a massacre
at her office.
One is the child
of a rape victim.

These are women
of the 20th Century.

Mother Saint

Mother is a saint
who lives in an old shoe.
She files her nails
with moonbeams,
moon song bellowing
through fire lit lips.
Mother is a saint.

Mother is a saint.
She pours round pennies
through arthritic fingers,
gently counting, gently
counting one for every day,
two for each child.

Mother is a saint.
She calls us home with
a brass gong,
round tones ring out of
Chinese scenes, five tiers
of floating farms.

Mother is a saint,
a sullen, sultry one
in youth,
hysterical
later on.
She held on
to the century
with broken fingers.

Mother is a saint,
churned butter and then
mixed yellow dye
with lard
when that ran out.
She took in sewing,
made clothing—beautiful
like she was.

Photo by James Dwight Safford

Endangered

They simply
drop
out of existence.

Hazel eyes, wild—
soft brown fur.
There are thirty Florida Panthers left
and they will die
unless they can be tricked into
breeding
in captivity—panthers
don't understand farms.

Puppy-faced water baby—
shark food.

The Hawaiian Monk Seal
gets caught in commercial
fish nets,
doesn't understand—
dies tangled
in fishing line.

Golden flash,
float past, winged alphabet.

Hurricane Andrew
and a century of pesticide
poisoning has killed
all but 100 Sachaus
Swallowtail Butterflies.

Speckled feathers,
duck face, goofy looking bird.

In 1923
there were twenty Laysan Ducks
left on earth.
Still that small flock,
on a single island
in Hawaii, is
one hurricane away
from extinction—
feather hunters.

Loudmouthed parrot
screeching at the Arizona Desert

The Thick-Billed Parrot
could fly 60 mph,
you could hear it's call
three miles away.
Listen—
we think they're gone.

Prehistoric giant, nine foot wingspan,
pointy, spine-headed grandmother—
please don't die.

There are 89 California Condors
and twenty million dollars worth
of captive breeding
can't bring them back.
People shoot them, or
they fly into telephone wires,
and there's poison everywhere.

One by one we go—

The Road from the House of the Mother

Highway 101 winding south to San Francisco down to the rainbow
tunnel and across the Golden Gate Bridge, superimposed on an image
that hangs in my mind—a photograph of the San Francisco Bay before
there were bridges, when you had to take a ferry from Oakland
to the City, from the City to Sausalito, when electric trains ran all
the way up to Santa Rosa, over to Napa, and Sonoma—an image of
the continent on the brink of the twentieth century. Photographs
flash back at me from 1915—Grandfather in Asia, Mother, an infant
in his arms. Grandmother and Mother in a rickshaw alongside the
Great Wall of China. The world changed.

Their victories turned grotesque, and the road home to the mother
was fractured—the farm in the mountains in Pennsylvania has become
a condo on the edge of the continent not far from the ocean where fog
buries everything, even our motives. The faces of those people in 1915
brimmed with optimism and radiant hope. They were passionately alive,
unknowingly falling over the edge of the most violent century in history.
Where did they bury the seed of that violence?
Grandfather was a missionary, Grandmother a nurse.
They weren't assassins.
The man pulling the rickshaw was a hundred and ten, had been running
through Chinese streets like a pony for a thousand years, in front of a wall
that was built to keep out barbarians, that was meant to keep in lace fields
floating down terraced mountainsides—and graceless oppression.

Photos by James
Dwight Safford

"Maude's Camel Train,

China, I think"

is what it says on the back of the photograph—
a wide panoramic black and white photograph
of the Great Wall of China, 1913, Grandmother
riding the tenth camel back, perched side saddle
riding a camel, a farm girl from *Up/State/NewYork*,
a new bride on her honeymoon camel.

Grandfather, head buried behind a fine Bausch & Lomb lens,
out of the picture, was lost to the shadows of death,
and Grandmother lived past his death, worked as a nurse—
sent two children to college, assisted a doctor whose wife
was a morphine addict, was the office masseuse,
grew eccentric with age, but not without telling the stories,
stories of another world, one she'd seen—
a world of camel trains and mosquito nets, bidets, appliqué,
cloth shoes, embroidery and Chinese silk.

She said Chinese women bound their feet
to be beautiful and were crippled.
She said everyone fussed over my mother's blond curls.
"Who was the photographer?" the children always asked.
"Dwight Safford," she said. *" liked to take pictures."*

Photo by James Dwight Safford

English as a Second Language

"Bocsanat" (sorry)
it says on a white index card
and beneath that
a sad face,
mouth curved down,
eyebrows drooping.
The card is taped onto the cabinet
over a red kitchen sink.
"Ehes Vagyo" (I'm hungry)
is taped to the side of the refrigerator,
overlapping collages of family photographs.
"Kavet"
is hung on the coffee maker
and it says *"Tegnap"* on the silver drawer.
I ask what *"Tegnap"* means
and she says *"Yesterday."*

"Why is it on the silver drawer?"
I ask Sara, who is twenty-two
years old. I remember when
she was born. Now she
is packing for a year
in Hungary.
She has been upstairs,
downstairs, downstairs upstairs,
a thousand times.
A few minutes ago
she was sitting cross-legged
in the upstairs bedroom with a pair
of socks in one hand and a postcard
in the other, short circuiting—
looking
from one to the other,
and back.
"Why is 'Yesterday' on the silver drawer?"
I ask her and she tells me,
*"If I put it on the calendar
I won't know what it means."*

Photo by James Dwight Safford

She hurries down to the basement
to bring up a load of socks.
Someone has told her
underwear is expensive
in Hungary.
Sara is a third generation feminist
moving into a new world.
It is very late. Her plane leaves
in the morning and she has lost
her ticket to New York.
She is worried.
"I don't know the language.
I will be teaching English to boys
at a military academy."
Her mother is phoning the airline.
"Ebed" it says next to a picture of food
and an early clock face.
"Reggeli," is written on a white card next to
a cartoon of hamburgers and a beer mug.
"Vacora" it says next to a sandwich on a plate.
"But I know how to learn.
I don't think I'll wear jeans the first day—
What do you think?"

Mother Cloud

You walk on my clouds,
reach for my hand
and the clouds are ideas
I call true.
Mother held me too,
the way I hold you.

I followed like you,
true to her voice
so the clouds
would maintain.
She held true.

I cannot hold
so well
onto you,
who cloudbursts
and falls through,
still so small.
Still so small.

I hand out
skill after skill,
feathers too,
but you fall—
like I do.

*"I think I going
to die too."*
But you don't,
bird child,
you ride clouds
I call true.

Photo by James Dwight Safford

26

Maude Safford, 1885-1967

It is 1915.
We are standing alongside the Great Wall of China. You are wearing a long linen gown. In your arms, a parasol and a naked baby, Mother. A rickshaw passes, frozen in the sepia tones of an old photograph. Grandfather is out of the frame. It is springtime in Manila. Mother is a toddler. She is wearing lace, sits in a fanback wicker chair next to a row of solemn dolls. *It is 1916.* Grandfather has sleeping sickness. It is 1890, you have taken off my emerald and opal ring to wash dishes. You have propped up a German book and study as you wash plates. *Upper/NewYork/State,* farm country. *It is 1951.* You and I are sitting in a metal swing chair. You have come to visit and I have climbed up to sit next to you. At first I don't recognize the house, then I see my window curtains. It is a simple white wood house, like the one I live in now. It is the next day. You are wearing a fancy dress. It is rayon and looks like Jackson Pollack painted a galaxy across your hips. I am listening to stories about the Philippines, how children slept under mosquito nets, how servants did the work, how mother played in the bidet, how Grandfather was the nicest man in the world. *It is 1968.* It is the end of summer and I am going back to college. We are having lunch in a Victorian restaurant on Lake Michigan. You are telling me to get the wagon and we'll go to town with your mother and father. I have learned to follow your time leaps. When I leave you, dress blowing, blue against whitecaps on the water, white hair blowing, knowing reaches out of your old face into my heart and I swallow the pain of our last hour together. *It is 1958.* You have come to live with us. Father has built a room addition. He digs dandelions out of the front yard with a sharp bladed trowel. You cook them for supper. We take walks and you tell me the names of the

Photo by James Dwight Safford

birds and the flowers. One day you walk to the next town. Father thinks you are trying to walk your-self to death. The man at the hardware store says you just walked up, seemed tired and sat down. The light headed forgetfulness, time slipping weirdness you teach me to love is hardening of the arteries. To me it seems wildly logical. *It is 1949.* We are in your room in your sister's house. Uncle John just showed me the Pennsyl-vania Dutch garden—compost, manure, brilliant color. The scent is strong and mixes with his sweat. Aunt Grace knows you and Mother but cannot remember whose child I am. You use jars of cold cream to prop up the window. I pull one out and smash my fin-gers. *It is 1910.* You are dressed in a wedding gown, v-neck, lace-draped, simple, long white gloves. The diamond pendant hangs round your neck. Three sparkling drops of light. You have packed trunks and are going to China. *It is 2010.* Mother and I visit you in a wall-papered room. You are sur-rounded by oriental fabric and china, vases and jars are filled with cream and scent. You are very old. We think it is fine that you are still dancing. We all dance. Moonlight is tinted and rose scented.

Photo by James Dwight Safford

Transcendental Elation

Mira Bai 1498-1573

"My love came
and vanished from my courtyard
while I was sleeping."

She was looking for someone to create for,
a god would do. The emperor was coarse, unfeeling,
sent her a cup of poison. Who needs that?
She was rash, prone to wild dancing, ecstatic vision.

"Mira is dancing with bells
tied on her ankles.
People say Mira has gone mad.

"Her mother-in-law is upset
at the ruined family honor."

Mira was passionately in love with a god,
one of the imaginary ones, who don't exist, who
die young, stretched across pain they didn't create.
She lay awake waiting to hear his voice,
a spray of wind brushed against the moon,
scent bursting from nowhere—
divine madness.

She was integrating the two sides of her soul
male/female, passive/active—
god/goddess—one dance,
understanding/passion, the star,
the eternal kiss, the way you look at me
sometimes and wonder—
"Is she capable of the god dance?"
Holy image twisting inside me like a snake
pointing to some part of myself.
The dance, the dance, bells tied to my heels.

The emperor sent her poison, her lover died,
but she was still alive, had a life to live,

anyway she could—
might have made baskets, sold them at market,
except she was a poet, entranced by a god,
who hovered, just past touch.

"Without him I can't rest,
but my heart is not angry.
My limbs are weak,
my lips call to him.
This pain of separation
cannot be understood.
I am like the rainbird calling for clouds."

Photo by James Dwight Safford

Drink from this Cup

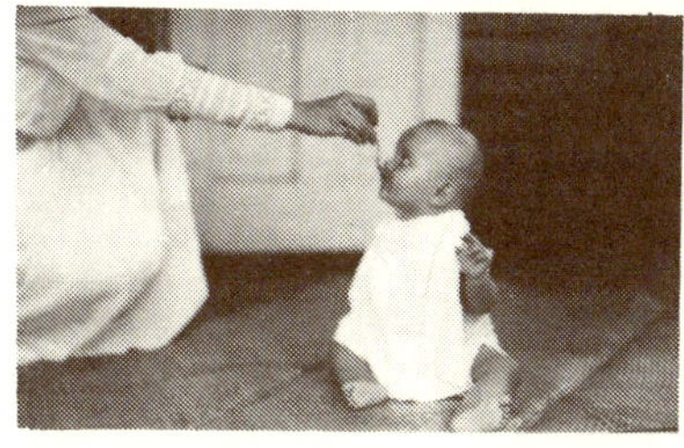

She is running, naked as the day you were born, leaping into the spiral at the end of her life, bridging your sky. A spectrum of the colors of mother explode like birdsong into the childplace. The unformed forces of us ripple in her wake, water of mother and infant, a slippery magnet. And the storms of our being undulate, lightning and thunder. There's a fire in the desert that she fans with her breasts. Children stretch into the future, cracking smartass jokes, smirking in disrespect. They have forgotten the holy circle, swallow a draught of forgetfulness equal to the time they need to leap into form. Mother is a full spring torrent, a river swollen to flood. She is washing away with the ancestral house, white wood, Victorian trim. She is picked up like a small child's toy, tossed, she rolls over a great damn exploding. Mother rolls back to her own life, having failed to raise the perfect child. This is necessary. These floods are her tears. Some of the children have died, some fall to despair, to violence, some fly into entropy or dissolve. A clown pulls families out of sane places, pulls their strings. Houses race up and down mountainsides that ought to be clouds. Fish from the valley swim up and swallow us whole. I am sunlight and fire and power. See how I climb up the dark mountain, reach out of sky to find you, to bridge for you the distance between this instant and the future. Relationship. That is her secret. See how all of the streets in the giant metropolis wind back to one house, house of the mother, home for the soul, center, beginning. This is the fact she carries in her side pocket, walking in the marketplace, sketching on a laptop computer, running a jack hammer, plowing a cornfield. Mother carries with her the center, at the same instant her own center doesn't exist, falls to zero. When she dies, they all come. Even then they don't know the scope of her power. Even when they suspect it, they are blind, so deeply have they swilled from her draught of forgetfulness.

Photo by James Dwight Safford

Rsella G. Weaver

Eugene Treat Smith

Hot Week

It was a hot week, July 5-11, 1880, Deposit, New York, "*the dog days, so called by the ancients because the dog star rose with the sun, causing a malignant influence,*" according to **The Deposit Courier**, published Saturday, July 10th in a one page edition, no room for advertisements, because "*A majority of our stock, press, type, paper, etc. is still on the road. Whether it will arrive for next week, we cannot say.*" ❋ In column one it is reported that "*Flagging for a new walk in front of the Catholic Church is being delivered;* ❋ *The yard on the east side of the Methodist church has been filled up and graded;* ❋ *The census of Deposit foots up to 1500, an increase*

of about 500 in the last five years; ❋ *Wickwire and Russell are filling up their old store;* ❋ *O.T. Bundy, M.D. has commenced to build an addition on the east side of his residence;* ❋ *A platform has been erected at the depot for the convenience of those who wish to alight from or take carriages there;* ❋ *Dr. L. E. Knapp has established his dental office in the rooms over Loder's store and has received his new tools;* ❋ *Many strangers have been visiting in town for the past two or three weeks, and owing to the pressure of work we have not been able to learn their names;* ❋ *Those interested in astronomy can see the new comet now in the heavens by looking to the left of the north star, and half way between it and the western horizon. Though faint, it can be distinguished by its train of light, and 11 o'clock is the best time to see it."* ❋ In the second column we learn that a correspondent from the other newspaper has suggested that Deposit *"don't need any fire department."* ❋ In the third column we read about two insurance fires. *"Deposit's noble and only volunteer fire brigade fell to work. Water was hard to get, but it came somehow, by the hands of women often, and soon the fire was mastered."* ❋ In the fourth column we learn about a temperance meeting at which the Reverend Thomas J. Whittaker of Franklin, being called for, spoke briefly showing that *"the chief enemy of temperance reform is the indifference of the people toward this great work."* ❋ We learn that "Mr. Wm. *Bushnell was almost killed by a tree falling on him;* ❋ *That a seven year old girl of Mr. Breflle, of South New Berlin, was fatally burned by the explosion of a kerosene lamp;* ❋ *That Mrs. Wm. Gray and her son James, aged about 15 years, were coming down the mountain road when their horse commenced kicking and ran away, throwing them both out. Mrs. Gray was badly injured, and her son was caught in the wheel and his head torn off, which of course killed him."* ❋ And we learn that *"a man by the name of William Easton attempted to commit suicide on Sunday evening in Norwich, Chenango County, by jumping into a barrel of water."* ❋ On the second page, which is the back of the front page, and which is also the last page of **The Deposit Courier,** are regional, national and world events, headlines without stories: ❋ *"Two million more taken off the national debt in June;* ❋ *One hundred and eighty thousand immigrants in six months and they still come;* ❋ *Russia has proclaimed a state of siege in the province bordering on China;* ❋ *Numerous deaths from sunstroke occurred in New York during the week;* ❋ *Nearly a hundred children died each day of cholera infantum;* ❋ *Heavy damage done to the richest farming lands of Illinois by the bursting of the Mississippi levees near Quincy. Thousands of acres inundated and a number of lives lost;* ❋ *Macon, Ga. reports the falling and near explosion of a meteor as large as a barrel;* ❋ *Census reports the United States has more than doubled in population in less than a generation."* ❋ We learn more about a new tobacco tax; and that ❋ *"a remarkable epidemic fell upon several towns in Western Massachusetts on the night of Tuesday, June 15 when out of a population of 6000, between 600* and 1000 people became prostrated by a disease resembling cholera." ❊ In what looks like a filler paragraph hand set in lead type and stored on the shelf until a space opened up, we learn. ❊ *"If a musket ball be fired into water it will not only rebound, but be flattened; if fired through a pane of glass, it will make a hole the size of the ball without cracking the glass; if suspended by a thread the thread will not even vibrate."* ❊ Then we discover that army worms have eaten the entire regional crop of hot house grapes, making a total failure of this *"delightful crop."* ❊ And there is a warning to bald-headed men who should, *"now that fly time has arrived, paint a spider on the exposed place to frighten away pests."* ❊ Finally, before two farm foreclosures and a summons for what looks like an entire family by the name of Brown, comes an announcement, starred and underlined in ink—certainly the reason this singular edition of **The Deposit Courier** stayed in my family for over a hundred years; ❊ *"Married, Smith—Weaver, in this village, at the house of Wm. Miller, June 15, by Rev. C. B. Landon, Eugene T. Smith and Miss Rose G. Weaver, both of Deposit."*

Maude in Photographs

—daughter of Rosella G. Weaver and Eugene Treat Smith, married, like
her mother in Deposit, New York. Maude Smith, born in 1884. On the
last day of her life, she returned to Deposit, telling her father to hitch up
the wagon so they could go into town, skin folding in halos on crackled
bones. In high school photographs she laughs like a pixie, making funny
faces, dressed in white organdy, hair pinned up, wisps of hair moving
with the wind, graceful and funny, a spark in her eyes, an *Upper/
NewYork/State* farm girl, photographed as a child outside the farm house,
leaning against Rosella's skirt, black boots, cotton stockings, wool dress
and a shawl, smiling like a wooden doll with rope curls. James Treat
Smith, long bearded and dark, standing close to Rosella, a hand on her
shoulder, squinting at the camera. Front door and windows open to the
air, geraniums on the windowsills, potted plants outside the front door,
the farmhouse scoured, tired and lean. The photograph is torn on one
edge now, cream colored with age. Maude Smith read the newspaper,
didn't marry until she was thirty, was an old maid, until she met Dwight
Safford at a church meeting. He worked for the YMCA—was going to

Photo by James Dwight Safford

China, was the most beautiful man she had ever seen. There was hope in him, and light. He photographed her in *Upper/New York/State* and in China. He photographed her playing with their baby, and he photographed the cottage they lived in. He photographed her in a rickshaw, and on a camel alongside the Great Wall of China. He photographed the army tent. She photographed him sitting in a camp chair, mother climbing onto his lap. He photographed the cornerstone of a Chinese temple and the fronds of a palm tree. He photographed Maude feeding mother, sequential takes, the baby passionate with laughter, hunger and life. Maude was laughing. Maude was spilling over with love, child/love, man/woman love, in light brimming with hope. He photographed fellowship workers in Manila, flowers and palm trees in the background—Maude passionately happy, grown mid-life into a flowering mother who learned to be a nurse overseas, who nursed Dwight until he died, leaving her a widow with two small babies. And she never married again. Maude to our cameras scowling, complaining, *"I always look terrible in pictures,"* was to his lens exact beauty.

Grandmother wrote on the back of this picture, *"An immodest picture of me in native clothing."* She is covered head to foot—perhaps it bothered her to appear without a belt.

Photo by James Dwight Safford

36

Mother Bright

"*At 1038 Woodlawn Street.
In the United States of America.*"

A Model T. Ford was parked alongside the house George May Cure Bright gave birth in, in a front room, bay window, lace curtains facing onto Woodlawn Street, a fine two-lane street stretching uphill to Washington Avenue—inside a woman pushing to childbirth. She was strong then, a concert violinist, before her heart gave way to Angina. She was young, lithe and graceful, later she called herself *Mother Bright*, here lying in childbirth, a Model T. Ford parked outside. Helen played alongside the bed my father was born in. A printed announcement "*Born to Mr. and Mrs. William Edward Bright on the fifth day of May in the year of 1914 in the City of Scranton, County of Lackawanna, State of Pennsylvania.*" and in Grandmother's hand "*in the United States of America at 1038 Woodlawn Street.*" Later she wrote: "*Baby's first outing—the 24th of May in the year 1914 by Papa in a Ford auto.*" And later—"*The baby calls himself* **Me**." In pictures, he looked like my sister. So did Helen. Father's Grandfather, the "*Reverend George Alvah Cure presided over the sacrament of baptism.*" John Cure, the banker, and Grandmother Helen Virginia Lewis Cure, who looked like my father, daughter of David J. Lewis, and Hannah Helen Hubbard were there too. Grandmother's slant hand recording child words: "*I like my letter book best.*" "*I'd go right to sleep if you'd tell me three stories in a row.*" "*Why am* **I** *me?*" Against white wood, the families line up for a picture. The Cure Brothers look like twins, black coats, tall men in top hats; and the Brights—William Senior, born in England, one of ten children, left school to work, became a blacksmith, came to America at seventeen, made casts for Dorflinger Crystal, opened a wagon repository and blacksmith shop; Grandmother Bright, Lucy A. Titus, daughter of Jedidah Bump Tiffany Titus, daughter of Captain Isaac Titus, a Quaker from *Up/ State/NewYork.* These people, a river in flood, pressing down on a woman howling in labor, in the upstairs front room, at 1038 Woodlawn Street, in the United States of America, a woman who was a musician, a concert violinist, who signed letters to us *Mother Bright.*

Rehoboth

On the northern coast of Africa, Abraham's children searched for water, but the desert people fought with them or filled the wells with sand. For many years it went like that—Abraham's children finding water, the desert people taking back their own, until one day a well was dug and no one noticed, or cared. Isaac named the land Rehoboth, place of peace. He said his people would stay there and plant. He said the land would bear great bounty, enough for everyone. And so the people lived to dream in peace of staircases leading up to heaven, lined with Ziegfeld angels. Jacob lay his head down on a stone that turned into Bathsheba which turned into something else. And Rehoboth which seemed like eternal peace was in fact more like the peak on one hill of a roller coaster that hadn't been invented yet. When Grandmother inherited the farm, three hundred years after the Indians had been banished from land they knew was their mother, it was already called Rehoboth, place of peace. And for a time it was a place of prosperity. Each generation added structures and then graves. The Cure brothers, children of the first John Cure, built the old barn, which is still standing, although the cabin is gone. They built a church and the small outbuilding next to it which became a library my grandmother called Rehoboth Storybook House. She hosted children's hours and concerts. Neighbors and family members played hymns and sang popular songs. My father was Thomas Jefferson in a play Grandmother wrote about freedom from racism, players calling to each other at the top of their lungs in a makeshift amphitheater, outdoors in the spring, to raise money for scholarships, children to be educated from the bounty of a place in the Allegheny Mountains where two roads met. Rehoboth was to be a retreat, an art school but the land slid out from under her children, in spite of the fact that they baked great holiday feasts, cracked jokes, told stories and filled concert halls in Pennsylvania and *Up/State/NewYork* with the songs of a thousand musicians. Rehoboth is fresh painted white and empty now, one instant in a fast carnival of intersections and highways, art and being smashed into great waves of howling feedback.

The Creek

"*Go down and look,*" Helen told me. Mother was 76, Helen 82, too old to climb down to the creek. So I found my way alone down to the water where we used to play as children. When father couldn't stand what was happening to him, I asked Helen what he loved, how to remind him of something good, to put next to the pain in his mind. "*Remind him of the creek, of when he was a boy,*" she said. So I told him, "*You don't have to stay here. Go back to the farm, to the creek, listen to the water run over gray stones, coal colored water. Remember the creek.*" That's how in his last few hours, some part of him came here. Sound first bonded me to the creek, and then plants, ferns and wild comfrey, wild flowers—*Trillium, Lilly of the Valley* (for which I am named), *Violets, Blue Gentians, Hepatica, Anemone*—and the deep carpet of leaf mulch, like walking on a mattress. Sinking ankle deep into this once, I reached for a walking stick that snapped and set me tumbling into the leaves and sticks and the rich smell of forest earth. I was listening to the sound of water running over stone. I was enchanted by the darkness of the forest, by splashes of sunlight that came through what Father called *windows* in the trees. Father said they cut windows in the forest to warm up the creek water where it flowed into a concrete swimming pool which Grandfather built alongside the main part of the creek. Father said it didn't help, that creek water was cold enough to wake the dead. Perhaps it had. I asked Helen what the creek was called. She said it didn't have a name, that it had just always been called *the creek.* I wonder if the land remembers us, knows our souls or the rhythm of our footfall. I wonder and am filled with wonder by this place that doesn't need a name.

Iris

The vibrance of the universe is so obvious it is difficult to
comprehend what could have led us from wide-eyed knowing
that it is alive.
From nucleus to cell wall is a trillion light years.
The blink of an eye contains the eternal reality of dream. In any tree
there are galaxies with comets flashing through wood like space.
Linear space/time is "A" not *"The"* dimension.
The translations we are incapable of are more thick than ants.
We can't even talk to fish.
The power to imagine is the power that radiates from star
to planet. I splash water on my face, drops fall on a galactic map
spread out beneath my feet.
Spiral galaxies form with red and living stars ready
to shoot patterns across my skin.
Piles of alphabets, icons, and the love between them
balanced on the rim of a crystal are the images
we have for the bath of universe we move through,
thinking we are earth people,
the illusion of our age,
Earth People,
soon to be condensed,
soon to be transformed.

Our children will wander space like we roamed creekbeds, stones
through our fingers: stars through theirs.
They will sleep, like we do, but with respect for both sides of
the veil.
The iris dilates—

Mother Fish

The swimmers,
the real ones
are clear
and emerald
like the water
that pulses
up from the center
of the planet
spinning
and cold.

They
blend with the water
so fast
you don't see them
except when
they get in
or out—
they are invisible
once they're
moving.

They dry off
quickly
and go
but the essence
stays with
them,
a glow
just below the surface
of the skin—
emerald light.

Maude notes that this is a double exposure. *"See the phantom ship,"*
it says on the back of the photo. These women weren't thrown
overboard, they are wearing swim dresses and caps. See pg. 28.

Photo by James Dwight Safford

Electric Street School # 27

Father was seven or eight before anyone realized he couldn't see. The
only birds he recognized were Cardinals. At school desks with book
shelves and ink wells were made of oak and wrought iron filigree, eight
desks to a row, five rows across. In Father's second grade picture, the
children's books are open, pads angled for writing, pencils poised. But
they look suspicious of the photographer. At the back of the room a large
eyed woman, hands on hips, stands scowling and brittle. The school was
an old factory thirty windows long, three stories high, with smoke stacks.
It was plain stone and bleak. Father's grandparents lived across the street
in a rambling wood house with a porch on two stories that curved
around to one side, a great house of porches, stately by our standards, but
then it was the home of a blacksmith and a school teacher. Father said
the teacher chewed snuff and stood, one leg propped up on a chair,

lecturing the class in between fast missals of spit she spewed into a spittoon that sat on the floor dangerously close to the children in the front row. Father was always in the front row, and until he got glasses wasn't much of a student. The classrooms were astoundingly dreary, chalk boards with endless lessons scrawled across them. Girls and boys both wore hightop black boots, laced tight. The boys wore short pants and stockings, the girls long, dark skirts and sailor shirts. All were dressed warmly. Winter light slanted through long rows of windows. The old school is abandoned now, boarded up, windows broken, overrun with weeds, trash blowing across the front steps. But in 1924 the children were scrubbed clean, pressed and starched. Their images where caught in sepia toned photographs, one for each child. It was a privilege to go to school, it always has been. In 1924 Electric Street School # 27 was dreary as oatmeal. But they lived in a boom town—the children, clear eyed and innocent, astride a fast tide of prosperity, manifest destiny, spittoons, black boots and chalk dust.

Girl Scout Camp

"When I was twelve, they made me go to
camp here in the woods. They wanted everyone
to do the same thing all the time, and
I was a foot taller than all the other girls.
We stayed in buggy cabins
and had to sleep in bunk beds."
Helen said.

"I loved it,"
said my Mother, who wasn't raised
in a twenty-eight room house on Washington Avenue,
whose father died when she was six years old,
who was raised by a single mother, who
lived in her sister's house, the husband a stern and foul
smelling Pennsylvania Dutchman who *"wore out his shoes*
walking all over town to save two cents on a bag of sugar."

"I loved camp." Mother said.
"I didn't have a beautiful summer home to come to.
It was the only time I got out of the city."

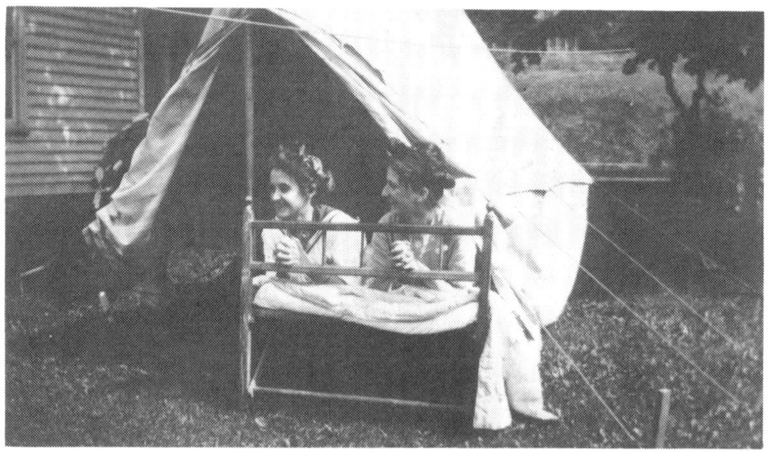

Photo by James Dwight Safford

44

Lemonade

After Father's family moved into the twenty-eight room house on Washington Avenue, the family rented out their Woodlawn Street house and one summer it was Father's job to paint it—a fine hot job for a young man back from college, who'd earned straight A's and consumed an astounding amount of expensive Scotch. Grandpa Bright believed children should work to maintain the family property and he paid them for it. He believed it made them resourceful, and it did. Grandpa, who never smoked and didn't take a drink until he was seventy, thought painting would be good for William, and it may have been, although it made him profoundly thirsty. He asked Anne to make lemonade, and since she'd have to walk three blocks downhill, two blocks over, two blocks back over and three blocks up—by which time the ice in the lemonade, ice was precious in 1934, would have melted—William gave her his car. She'd driven a few times with supervision and protested appropriately, but he was thirsty and sure she'd be fine. Two blocks downhill weren't much trouble—a little coasting and steering at just the right time. And one block over wasn't hard. She made the downhill trip, made the lemonade, fresh squeezed, using every particle of lemon, rind and all, ice and sugar, and then she placed, carefully, two glasses and a pitcher on the floor board of the passenger side of William's car. She drove one block over fairly well, although her toes just touched the petals. But as she was about to make the turn onto Woodlawn Street, she realized the lemonade would spill if she didn't reach down to hold it straight, which she did—and in so doing veered strangely up to the front porch of the house on the corner of Boulevard Avenue and Woodlawn Street, at the exact instant Grandfather was making, rather more precisely, the same turn from the opposite direction, on his way back to the Greenridge Bank, where he was president, four blocks over and three more blocks down. He tipped his hat and said, *"Good afternoon Anne. Hot day, isn't it."*

Fieldstone Fireplace

In the cabin where I was born, Father built a tall fieldstone fireplace. The floor was fieldstone too and walls were lined with triangle bookcases molded to the shape of the corners of the room. The fireplace was large enough to cook a goat in but no one ever thought of that. Wood burned hot to ash in that fireplace, wood that Charlie and George cut in the summer—Charlie, a school teacher who needed to keep busy in the summer, and George who would rather have done almost anything else. It was harvest wood from dark green forest land where splashes of light nourished pockets of wild flowers, where creek beds were lined with ferns, and fieldstone jutted out of layers of leaf mulch two feet thick. It was a cabin full of books: **The Flowering Earth**, (Donald Culross Peattie, 1939, Putnam and Sons) a book about *"Ecology, loosely defined as the sociology of plants;"* **Providence as Manifested Through Israel, an Address to the Descendants of Abraham.** (Boston, Leonard C. Bowles, 1833) *"a discourse on Christian Unitarianism connecting Islamic, Judaic and Christian thought;"* **Leaves of Life, for Daily Inspiration** (Margaret Bird Steinmetz, Abingdon Press, 1913) *verses from the Bible for daily meditation;* **Green's History of the English People, Volumes I-X**, *early evidence of Father's passion for history;* **Poe, Complete Works,** (Walter J. Black Co., 1927) cloth bound, foil stamped, malachite marbled end papers; **Love-Lyrics,** (James Whitcomb Riley, with *'Life Pictures'* by William B. Dyer, The Bowen-Merril company, 1899, cloth bound, foil stamped) *love poetry and photographs;* **Green Fields and Running Brooks** (James Whitcomb Riley, The Bowen-Merrill Company, 1892) *"All unsung of words or books, / Sing green fields and running brooks!" Narrative*

farm poems written in country dialect a hundred years ago. **The Poems of Henry Wadsworth Longfellow** (Thomas Y. Crowell Company, 1901) *"To Anne, with love from Mr. and Mrs. Wm. E. Bright and George C. Bright, May, 1937."* Longfellow, the Harvard poet, husband to an heiress, the poet of high culture; a **Hebrew and English Lexicon of the Old Testament,** (Crocker and Brewster, 1854) with a note inside dated, May 1876. *"Sold my 'short breeches' to Geo. Norman (janitor) and he exchanged his wife's wash bill with Johnny for this book. It cost $4.00."* It was a tall fireplace on the far wall of a room lined with books. Heat was radiant, warming fieldstone which warmed the air it touched creating warmth in a cabin further insulated by the passion of the mind.

Marigold

Past the porch door of an old
mountain cabin
I could see her red gold hair catch
sunlight
like a halo.

I watched her cross a meadow—
entranced by flashes of white golden
light
dancing around her.

And I knew, squinting, to hold the
image—
there in the mountains—this was
the last
I'd see of her.

Not even a meadow of angels in
starlight
could take the place of this girl
in my heart.

Cameo

That Jefferson Benjamin Franklin mistook his father for a pot roast in San Francisco is a story fit for telling after lunch to a table full of psychiatrists, who half-listen until the strangeness of it alarms them. Benjamin even then was old and rotund and Jefferson Benjamin was a mistake, *errata* is what Benjamin called the errors he made, times he veered from his schedule, the list of things he did every day—arise at five, meditate, write, breakfast, work till noon, accounting during the lunch hour, work, walk, supper, work, bed at ten. Benjamin accomplished a lot: the first postal service; he got street lights in Philadelphia lit before dawn; began the first library; the first bank; and the first hospital. He helped draft and he signed the *"Declaration of Independence."* All that even though he spent a fifth of his adult life in Europe instigating revolution. But he made mistakes. It was a French restaurant. The entree was *boeuf au jus* and he was the *boeuf*, had excused himself just before the main course to die which accomplished they laid him out in the kitchen, as then was custom. One thing led to another, exact facts, the order of events at this point speculation, Jefferson Benjamin Franklin waited as long as could be expected for Benjamin to return and then chose to go ahead and eat, supposing his famous father to be otherwise engaged, which in fact was the case, and when the great person arrived, *au jus*, neatly roasted, garnished with parsley, Jefferson Benjamin can hardly be blamed for not recognizing him. Nor can the chef, this was neither Philadelphia nor Paris, but the cuisine was excellent in San Francisco even in the late seventeen hundreds which was the time this culinary anomaly occurred, though we seldom read of it, it happened exactly like this—Jefferson Benjamin Franklin took a loaf of bread out of his pocket, sopped up the *au jus* and tore at the beef with his teeth, strong teeth, neatly placed. It was a cameo, an historical moment, a sliver of time, the day Jefferson Benjamin Franklin dined with his father in a French restaurant in San Francisco, high on a hill, and fog rolling in.

Tillie

The soldier's mother in New Milford, Pa.
walks across the village green to put new candles
in the Methodist Church.

We stop to visit on the 7-ton bridge,
an old fashioned two-lane bridge.

She is clear eyed and clear minded
this soldier's mother, the fabric
of American society—
worried that a florist charged too much
for a small bouquet.

"But they're orchids, They bloom once
in seven years, sometimes less than that.
This one smells like vanilla."

"I won't complain then," she says,
"I won't say anything about it."

Vanilla, earth sweet like the scent of a child
back from play on a hot summer day.

I look at her, standing on the bridge
and think America is formidable indeed.

Photo by James Dwight Safford

Both Hands

*"I wanted you to know what I sounded
like when I could really play."*

We were listening
to a tape recording
she'd made forty years earlier,
Bach, Scarlatti and Brahms
on the great pipe organ
at St. Luke's Church,
the installation of which
turned Helen
from the Methodist Church
where the Brights
and the Cures had
always gone, to St. Luke's
Episcopal Church.
Helen was a musician,
not a theologian.

"How did you play so many notes?"

There were more notes than I could listen to
but she could, fingertips fluttering,
feet tapping, head following intricate
lines of music she'd played long ago.

"How did you play so many notes?"

*"With both hands.
And both feet."* she told me.
"And both heads."

Nice Jump Grandma

After her fourth hip replacement operation
Hellie refused to admit she couldn't walk,
moved about at 82 with dauntless courage,
tipping over, sometimes falling down.

Once she fell down in the back yard
and the neighbor children picked her up,
all six feet long of her.

She wrote songs for fathers' poems
and produced a recital and reception for
two hundred people.

"How do you do it?" Mother asked,
and Helen said, *"I just don't care
how much it hurts."*

She moved with original free-form-fall
from one hand hold to the next,
using the strength of her shoulders and arms.

She'd make it to the hydraulic chair, pivot
on her good leg then free fall in, and bounce,
all six feet long of her.

And the grandson, who was six-four,
and played basketball, would say,
"Nice jump, Grandma."

Helen's Song

Plain, straight and simple,
white pointing steeple
   "Come to the church
    in the wild wood."
Mother's favorite hymn.

On a hilltop in the foothills—
one plain church, exactly elegant,
white against green forest,
pointing to God.

In the village velvet carpet grass
rolls from one threshold to the next,
no fences—
towering pines, hardwood maples
tuck houses into rich black earth,
root them there.

Helen plays the organ for the church.
Her fluid fingers find the chords—
choir songs reach out and up to *God*—
who lives here, in Penn's Woods—
a god I have no use for.

Still my soul vibrates to these songs,
to brilliant emerald and gold forest light,
to cool, earth smelling shadows, to the low
steady voice of mountain fern, the hilarity
of creek water running over stone,
and Helen's fingers moving over ivory keys
fill me with enormous love.

Jedidah Bump Tiffany Titus

was Hellie's great
grandmother, four foot tall,
quizzical looking
in the daguerreotype.

She was born Jedidah Bump,
married a Tiffany,
who died,
then she married a Titus—
Jedidah Bump Tiffany Titus.

"She'd be alive today,"
Hellie said,
*"if she hadn't fallen
down the stairs
when she was 96."*

Current Events

Great-grandmother Cure taped newspaper on the windows
at the farmhouse and on the windows in the 28 room house
on Washington Avenue because she was alarmed by ghosts
who were peering in at her. Father said she was crazy.
He said the children followed her around taking current events
off the window glass and got paid to do it.

Four small markers in the graveyard in Tomkinsville—

Martha, Mary, Ruth and John,
ages three to eight, four children who
died in March and April of 1885.

Diphtheric Croup. Bad water.
It made their throats fill up with
mucous so they couldn't breathe.

George May Cure was the only child who survived.
Father said she was too intense—
her own mother, *"mad as a bat,"* so many women thought mad.

Helen said, *"Grandmother Cure was the bravest woman I know."*

House on the Mountain

The porch, driveway and yard
were dark, but the rooms were full
of music and out back
an alley led to a penny candy store
where children bought
Mary Jane caramel by the fistful.

The attic was dark where the children
slept, innocent and peaceful,
on army cots from World War I,
hard beds where the covers didn't stay
tucked in, bristling blankets, army
green over crisp white sheets.

At night, Mother came up and sang and sang until
one by one the children dropped off—into cold,
dark mountain air where starlight whistled.
It was an unconscious house—

where girls were afraid of the boy's room, and boys
were afraid of each other, where men died young in the mines
or in American wars. It was a house that writhed
with cancer as if a house could inhale the dark mountain mist.

It was a house in a city that was built on a mountain
scoured hollow, and then set on fire—a fire that burned
for a century and dust on the china cabinet was black.
It was a house that knew agony and death and to spite that—

the most elegant music imaginable. It was a house
that sang and sang and sang. It was a house full of jokes
and welcome cups of the draught of forgetfulness,
where the mother perfectly overlooked everyone's faults—

perfecting just the best in each child. And the ones
who survived filled her grandmother house with grandchildren
and great-grandchildren who took music lessons and beat
each other up in the pasture outside of town.

Photo by James Dwight Safford

The Echo Window

was upstairs, in the farmhouse, a morning
window to open and call out—*"Susan."*
"Susan" would echo back in my exact voice.
"Mother. Mother" would call back.

Grandmother taught us the echo song:
"Little Sir Echo, / how do you do?
Hello, hello / hello, hello.
Little Sir Echo will answer you—
Hello, Hello, / HellO, / HELlo.
Won't you come over and play? / and play?
You're a nice little fellow I know by your voice,
but you're always so far away. / Away."

To a child this was a miracle, another self—
outdoors, a self that was the mountain.

Crescent Moons

I was dreaming of two sunsets, two *Suns*, and then three
like flaming speckled eggs slivered by *Moons* slipping
in front of them. I was dreaming of a flaming sunset
above a city that burst into quicksilver firework
explosions behind which nothing changed—fireworks
elbowing out of shrimp boats, fishnets winged on slate
blue water that mirrored double explosions—
millions of *Moon* crescents, pin hole *Moon* shadows
raining down like soft hail, dancing under trees beneath
shrubbery where song birds, cardinals, blue-billed ducks,
bull jays—song/hushed, roosted in darkness
where daylight belonged. Nature tells us what to do.

And I am just a poet, so when *Moon* crosses the path of *Sun*
at noon, I search the ground for crescent *Moons*, pin hole
illusions that dance in nonsense pleasure which I know exists—
cloud blankets can't hide it from imagination.
When *Sun* sets at high noon, then bounces back again,
we have to look beyond the clouds we cast out to defend
us from a vein of madness—hot moving to scour our planet
clean, when already it is a gleaming miracle.

Photo by James Dwight Safford

Hellie's Bible

Hellie keeps two songbooks from the seventeen hundreds
and the Bible Grandfather gave her at Confirmation
in a clear plastic bag which she keeps in the middle
drawer of a highboy in the red upstairs bedroom—
and elocution exercises.

She has been folding keepsakes
into the pages of this Bible for eighty years:
A letter from my uncle's widow explaining why
he committed suicide. Hellie says it leaves out things—
"Jacob's Ladder" by Denise Levertof *"I keep it to remind me
that a word can hold a thousand ideas."*

Hellie wants to know why I don't believe in God.
*"Don't you want some organizing principle, something
that holds everything together?"*
"Christianity is sexist."

George May Cure Bright with her mother Helen Lewis Cure holding William.
Lucy Titus Bright is seated next to Helen.

"Not at it's best." she says.
"I believe in ethics and community and holiness."
"But not in God?"
"No, not in God."

There is a letter my father wrote in the fifties
to set out his theory of *successful failure*—
he failed to accomplish the art his mother
expected of him, but made a lot of money,
becoming the most successful failure imagination
could envision. Hellie said he was contrapuntal.

"I've been stuffing things into this Bible
for so long the pages are falling out."

There are tongue twisters—
"A tooter who tooted the flute
tried to tutor two tooters to toot
Said the two to the tooter
is it harder to toot
or to tutor two tooters to toot."

A list of Georges—
"There is my mother, George May Cure
and my husband's father George
and my grandfather George
and my husband's grandfather George
and my second cousin George
and my son George and my grandson
George, who is an auto mechanic."

There are words to a hymn about violets
and forgiveness written in Great Grandfather's
handwriting and folded into the old hymn book.
There are flowers folded into psalms, flowers from weddings,
funerals, graduations, flowers from the high meadow at the farm.
Hellie folded a lifetime into the book of the family.

Providence

Yesterday Carol and Helen played
at the Methodist Church in Providence
where Great Grandfather Cure was minister
from 1900-1904. Helen played the piano.
Carol played Grandmother's violin.

The violin is important.
*"Mother played a concert in Providence
on that violin the day she died.
She went back home and played
duets with a friend for another hour,
set down the violin,
called out to Grandpa once, and fell.
Then she was gone."*

"Do you remember how they met?"
"They met at the parsonage, next door to the church."

*"Reverend Cure always asked my mother to entertain
the children of his visitors. He called up to her,
'George, come down and meet the Bright children.'
So down the staircase she came that day in 1902,
a box of toys in her arms. She stopped in the den
but there were no children.*

*"'Where are the Bright children?' she asked and up stood
William, 18 years old, 6 feet tall, the Blacksmith's son.
Oh they fought. Mother had an awful temper.
But she wouldn't admit it. She called it
'being emphatic.' They loved each other fiercely."*

"What did they fight about?"
*"They fought about everything.
They even fought about where the front gate was."*

"Did anyone go out and look?"
"No."

Grandmother was sure I'd make a great violinist. We posed for this snapshop
before the reality of having a tone deaf granddaughter hit her.

Real Estate

Standing in the sky,
my grandmother and I—

They are remodeling Helen's cabin by leaving it alone
to live in while they add on to the backside—
a great house, three stories high with long vaulted rooms.
But they cut down the trees—
You can see a great knot of cedar root and scrub maple,
sheet rock and construction refuse mixed in a soggy heap
blocking the Indian path across land no one owned.

A luxury home mushrooms out of the old cabin.
The new owner put stuffed chairs and a TV in the rafters,
so he can sit with his young wife and look at the bird nests.
But the songbirds are dying—one Oriole today
for every ten when Grandmother listened to their song.

"This land must remain in the family," she said—
Grandmother, who refused to cut down
a single tree, and built odd shaped houses
that made everyone laugh.

Standing in the sky, my grandmother and I—
She had plans for that land—a library called Rehoboth,
and a school—the great books, music, poetry and art.
"I've always thought the Cure
Barn would make a good school."

These dreams cracked like a large egg on the planet,
fractured—
so that her children and grandchildren accomplished
the vision, but did not hold the land. Now it's real estate.

Cornerstone

I thought it was the cornerstone
Grandfather built to hold
a lock box which held the family
history, but in the haze of dream
it's difficult know where you are and the
marker was covered with tall ferns.

Tall ferns pushed aside, the stone turned
out to be my brother's grave which
turned out to be a nursery full of toys,
alphabet blocks, pictures he had drawn,
and a flying horse that leaped out
of a window full of leaded glass, carved
oak and light.

One of the pictures was a child smiling,
standing in a field,
rainbow overhead, rabbit and zebra at his side.
I thought of my brother laughing.

Past the toy room was a subterranean mansion with oriental carpets,
ornate furnishings, gilded clocks, scales and balances,
art from every century, Tiffany lamps, cut glass and light
pouring in from the center of the planet, molten light.

And I have always known if I go through these rooms exhaustively,
in one of them will be the answer. Grandmother will have it.
She will be in the music room.

There will be light in her eyes and incredible sound will leap
from her fingers. It will be music poured from the soul of woman,
manifested in real things like the school she intended to build,
or the library she called Rehoboth.

Grandmother will have the answer.
She will be in the music room.

Crone

I remember the girl who was afraid of her own beauty.
I remember the woman who miscarried two pregnancies
and then a life she hated.
I remember the passionate artist who fell hard onto
the jagged edges of an assassin.
I remember a woman who picked herself up
and created a life that worked.
I remember a woman who walled herself up.
I remember a gentle love that endured.
I remember the mother fighting for the life
of a child.
I remember the activist insisting on sanity.
I remember a small girl, a woman past child bearing
mourning, mourning.
I remember reaching for a thread of courage
to admit beauty, to endure passion, to change culture,
to heal pain.
I remember these things, over and over, over and over
for centuries.

Tea Party

At the beach I threw two tea bags into
bottled water
and found Ann Bradstreet selling tea,
copyright long gone,
along with the privacy she required to
survive.
Her words set in cozy type in a pastoral
landscape
beneath cellophane—

"My head, my heart, mine eyes,
my life, nay more,
My joy, my magazine of earthly store,
If two be one, as surely thou and I."

"She was talking about her husband.
It's a love poem, has nothing to do with
drinking tea.
He was away, she said her bed was cold without him—"
My husband was setting out his fishing gear.
"I can't believe you know that."

It was good tea.
Set out in the sun, it roasted mellow, refreshed exactly
the sand parched August afternoon.
She wrote *"The Tenth Muse, Lately Sprung Up In America,"*
the first book by an American poet, rough poetry, homespun.
When her house burned down, along with everything she owned,
she stood among the ashes and said—

"Yea, so it was. So it was just."
She was modest, calling her work—
"Thou ill-formed offspring of my feeble brain."
She was realistic about her place in society—
"I am obnoxious to each carping tongue
Who says my hand a needle better fits;

A poet's pen all scorn I should thus wrong,
For such despite they cast on female wits;
If what I do prove well, it won't advance.
They'll say it's stolen, or else it was by chance."

Born in England, she survived smallpox, married at sixteen,
arrived in the New World when she was eighteen—

"I found a new world and new manners
at which my heart rose."

She was a Puritan woman, wife and daughter of men
who were Massachusetts Bay Colony governors.
She raised eight children in a frontier village.

Anne Bradstreet (1612-1672)—
a box of tea tossed sidelong in our camp box
half filled by noon with sand.

Women's Work

I can't imagine being able to get done
what I have to do today. It is impossible.
Guests will arrive to a house which has not been
cleaned in a month and the roses need water.

Students will not get papers back this week, or next.
I don't have time to get the car serviced or even vacuumed.
I have to pay bills, drop off art work, deposit checks,
pick up a check, deposit more checks.

I have to clean the bathroom and fold laundry.
I have to get something faxed and go to the post office.
I have to go grocery shopping, spend time with my child
after school—then cook supper while I drive to the ranch.

I have to do my income tax by tomorrow and there is no dog food.
Tomorrow there is no time either, and then we go on a trip
for which there is no time to pack. There isn't enough money or time
to figure out how much more money we need. Fleas are hatching.

In this chaos I have to find a way to do what I can
and not let the hungry mouths of unfinished work
scream at me! *"Now, now! My turn, my turn!"* Days like this,
months, years, decades have buried women for centuries.

I am buried like the grandmothers were—no, deeper.
Even though I thought it would not happen to me, it has.
Rude mouths of everything I can't do scream at me
even from sleep.

A Thousand Grandmothers

"They tell us we mistake our sex and say:
Good breeding, fashion, dancing, dressing, play
Are the accomplishments we should desire;
To write, or read, or think, or to inquire
Would cloud our beauty, and exhaust our time,
And interrupt the conquests of our prime;
Whilst the dull manage of a servile house
Is held by some our utmost art, and use.
Sure 'twas not ever thus, nor are we told
Fables, of women that excelled of old;
To whom, by the diffusive hand of Heaven
Some share of wit and poetry was given."

My mother lived under a dark cloud, and hers did too,
cloud of two world wars, grief for the father, then the son,
disease and mental illness, Ann Finch called it *spleen*,
Ann Finch, grandmother to a thousand poets
to whom her words were lost—
poets like Sylvia Plath, college actress for the part
of *Phoebe Clinket*, the play by Alexander Pope, written to poke
fun at Ann Finch, play daggers pointed at her spleen satirizing
"blue stocking" poets—how idiotic for women to write—he called
Ann Finch a *"Speaking Ass."* For Ben Johnson women writers were,
"after all like dancing dogs, the wonder is not that they do it poorly,
but that they can do it at all." Sylvia Plath, blonde glamour poet—
head stuck in the oven. Anne Finch called it *spleen*.

"A calm of stupid discontent,
The, dashing on the rocks, wilt rage into a storm.
Trembling sometimes thou dost appear,
Dissolved into a panic fear;
On sleep intruding dost thy shadows spread,
Thy gloomy terrors round the silent bed,
And crowd with boding dreams the melancholy head;
Or, when the midnight hour is told,
And drooping lids thou still dost waking hold,
Thy fond delusions cheat the eyes:

Before them antic spectres dance,
Unusual fires their pointed heads advance,
And airy phantoms rise.

She was Maid of Honor to the Dutchess of York,
was married to a good man—
"They err," she said,
"who say that husbands can't be lovers."
Wordsworth said she wrote the first original images of nature
in a hundred years. Ann Finch, woman poet of the sixteenth century
was depressed—

"My lines decried, and my employment thought
An useless folly, or presumptuous fault:
Whilst in the Muses' paths I stray,
Whilst in their groves, and by their secret springs
My hand delights to trace unusual things
And deviates from the known, and common way. . ."

One woman in ten thousand could read. For that one woman
to write poetry, to speak out in court was blasphemy—

"I was not so far abandoned by my prudence as, out of
mistaken vanity, to let any attempts of mine in poetry show
themselves while I lived in such a public place as the court,
where every one would have made their remarks upon
a versifying Maid of Honor, and far the greater number
with prejudice, if not contempt."

Ann Finch, woman poet, object of ridicule, scorn, shame—
retired from the court, in a bad mood her entire life, fell into melancholia,
her words fell too into a darker pit, into oblivion—

"a thousand pities that her mind was forced
to such anger and bitterness." (Virginia Woolf)

A thousand pities, a thousand grandmothers.

Children Have Souls

George could remember my
brother even though
I couldn't, was older, said they
tried to protect us,
but he knew something was
wrong, first a bandaged arm, then
long visits to the doctor,
then the hospital where George
went to visit.

He remembered that Tyke had to take pills
as big as his hand. George always wondered
how he got them down.

One day when George was playing
on the sun porch next to white wicker furniture.
He remembers that Helen brought in new clothes—
new clothes for a child to be buried in.

I asked Mother if I ever went to the hospital.
"You were too little," she said.

Once I read that until quite recently, anesthetics
were not given to infants. They didn't think babies
could feel pain. Of course we know that's wrong.
We know now that children have souls,
that their pain lasts all their lives.

Tunnel

I remember a light brown flannel tunnel
rolling into the sun,
west, from the mountains in Pennsylvania to
the rolling hills
of Illinois, from the cabin in the woods down
from Grandmother
and the farmhouse, from Helen's cabin, from
the creek—
to a neighborhood of tacky houses where I
learned fast not to trust
anyone. It was a light brown flannel tunnel, a
lumpy car
with a child's seat up front Mother called the
"Chicago seat."
We were running from my brother's death, we
were running
from Grandmother, we were spiraling into a
light brown tunnel,
an old lumpy car, a Hudson.
I remember mother's arm over the wide front seat.
Sometimes she would reach back to pat my knee—
We were floating west—
manifest destiny, the great migration.
Sometimes I rode between them.
It was summer. Grief was heavy in the air.
We glided past cityscapes and over farmland.
We tunneled into great fields of corn with fat golden nuggets
that burst between our teeth, sweet yellow juice—
We were hovering in a light brown flannel tunnel that
burrowed into the center of America.

Arrival

Smack at the center of America, on the Northern Illinois
shore of Lake Michigan is the house I grew up in.
A willow Father planted next to the septic tank
shades two backyards, and the garage needs paint.
Smooth concrete on the front porch is cool to our feet
and the windows are open—everything in place.
The downtown beach is a row of abandoned factories,
cracked glass windows are taped up. A *Space for Lease*
sign is blowing now where we used to swim.
Cut into the lake bluff, a freeway to Chicago
fans out to eight lanes—over passes, under passes.
Seventy percent of downtown is boarded up.
Grass grows through cracks in the sidewalk.
There is a Mexican grocery store on Genesse Street
and a *panderia* across from the high school.
The gas station attendant, a hollow eyed girl,
works behind bullet proof glass—everywhere danger.
Tacked onto the outskirts of town is the largest
discount mall in America—everything cheap.
Next to that there is a giant amusement park
called *Great America*—everything fun.
At the State Park in Zion, the beach is deserted.
Three hundred empty parking places stretch up to
yellow plastic tape around an abandoned luxury condo,
six stories high, beside which a half-dozen teenage girls
walk on the beach—next to the nuclear power plant.
I was one of those girls.

Sally

In dream there is a gaggle of children.
She bends to one, who signs *"I love you,"* and her song is gone.
When I catch word of her, it's from the ones who have not
forgiven her for leaving, with a shoe salesman,
pregnant, during her first year in college.

Mother said it didn't matter. *"She is still our friend."*
Her own family declined the wedding shower
Mother held in Sally's honor, after which
Sally left the Midwest for good.

I knew her real mother, though few people did,
and no one spoke of it.
I remember a gentle mother stretched long
on a turquoise couch in the living room before a wall
of windows gleaming out to the woods.

We cut paper dolls, and played on chocolate stone tile
floors set over hot water pipes for radiant heat.
I remember a mother who was dying, and then gone.
Sally got another mother who didn't look like her,
but she was kind to us, two small girls inventing lives.

We were ranchers in the Southwest. Sally woke at dawn
and galloped around the corner to my house.
By nine we were long gone to Arizona.
I liked her to sing for me and she would, while I listened,
until she grew self-conscious. Her voice was perfect.

Tuning Fork

Mother and Father
rang
true.

*"It is not
enough,"*
they taught us,
"to be beautiful,

*You have to ring
clear,
sound—
like a tuning fork."*

Photo by James Dwight Safford

Girl of Summer, 1957

The first breath of summer was sweet—
a girl moving across lush green
carpet grass in cool morning sunlight,
dew soaking new white canvas shoes,
the weight of school at bay,
she went out to play
and there were other children
with the same idea.
Behind every screen door
was a mother with cool drinks or
games to spread out, and rules—
"Cross your legs when you sit."
or first aid, iodine and gauze.
Fathers returned to the
neighborhood at night.

The girl of summer went from house to house
in a community isolated from almost
every social issue, protected from everything
except—
the stern community eye-balling
her to see if she was going
to be a mother, teacher or whore.

It looked like a close call. She was pretty.
Already there were gangs of boys lurking in the alley
to see what she was made of.

Big Top

Under the bigtop of the Barnum and Bailey Circus, Father sat with four eighth grade girls, five rings going—clowns and aerialists, spinning galaxies of mirrored light, jugglers and a pungent spiral of elephants. He asked if we were having a good time. It was the kind of thing his father did for children—haul a car load of them to New York City, after work, for a late supper, and a floor show, *Hells-a-poppin'*, then a show at Radio City, then a movie, then a quick breakfast before a fast drive back to Pennsylvania so he could open up the bank at 10 am. Father followed step, if more modestly. One event at a time was his style, but he found the good ones, less often in New York, though he took us there—once to see *Hello Dolly* with Ella Fitzgerald and Cab Calloway—but more often to Chicago. We heard Al Hirt at Ravinia, and saw *Hedda Gabbler* at the Goodman Theater. We walked on State Street under Christmas lights, and wandered for hours among the mummy cases at the Museum of Science and Industry—then stood beneath the giant swinging pendulum, dizzy as the spinning Earth. And under the big top once he asked my friends and I if we'd like to get together again, for another circus, in thirty years. We marked our life calendars, *"the Circus with Mr. Bright—distant future,"* but time/place fractured. He was in California, I was in New England, Sally was living in a trailer in New Mexico, Ann was ensconced in Midwestern academia. I haven't a clue where Ann's cousin went. When Father died, we taped the memorial service and sent copies to twelve states and two continents.

Chain of Lakes

Rest Lake, Clear Lake, Island Lake, Lake Star Light
Birch bark paper for letters home
from camp in the North Woods—

Dead Pine Lake, Wild Rice Lake, the Manitowish River
Children in bunk beds for afternoon naps
quiet hour, full of giggles and occasionally, sleep.

Manitowish Lake, Elkerson Lakes, Lower Gresham Lake,
Loud speakers blasted *"Rock around the Clock"*
at dawn to wake campers in cabins named—

Winnebago, Lac du Flambeau, Memoninee, Oneida
Mohican, Iroquois, Chippewa and Sioux, who
except for moccasins, had disappeared from

the *Northern Highland American Legion State Forest.*
Upper Gresham Lake, Diamond Lake, Trout Lake, Allequish Lake.
If you could swim across *Rest Lake* you could go on the canoe trip—
with gloves and a duffel bag, sleeping bag and a tooth brush,
three to a canoe, you learned a gently balanced leapfrog
to change positions, and you oared from lake to lake

in the clear Northern summer, gloves to protect child hands
from blisters. We circled campfires to sing hilarious songs
about naked bars of soap and birds dropping whitewash in your eye.

We bathed in the lake and scrambled in and out
of cat tails and poison ivy patches. We were children.
We camped on islands small enough to toss a stone across.

Counselors were rosy cheeked, strong boned and said
they liked to see the children smile. Silver water sparkling
in morning sunlight—hot by noon.

Mrs. Gravelhead

Mrs. Travelstead, we called her Mrs. Gravelhead, held court in the last room down at Greenwood Elementary School, last stop before junior high. At the end of fifth grade she came to speak to our class saying, *"I know you are shaking in your boots, but I promise you nothing is as bad as what they say about my sixth grade class. So have a good summer and come back prepared to work, work, work."* She said this in front of the fifth grade teacher, Miss Blimp, whose name was really Miss Flint, a whiny, timid woman whose sweat was rancid. Mrs. Gravelhead didn't sweat. We did. She put us to work, learning everything we'd missed, writing and performing plays and leading discussion groups which were particularly odd because no one shared new information. No one said, for instance, *"I have breasts."* or *"What am I supposed to do with this new dick?"* Bucky Broomstead, for example, had been telling us since third grade that he'd gone to a telephone conference and had been congratulated on his dialing. Mrs. Travelstead's plays were the only exciting thing I remember in elementary school. They were soap operas which Mrs. Travelstead said were so named because they were performed on soap boxes. That seemed odd to me. Our play was about the Aho family, which wasn't disrespectful because they were an actual family. I played the part of Mr. Aho and wore my band uniform—black pants and a white boy's shirt. There is a picture of me laughing at the audience laughing at me. I had attended no rehearsals because of whooping cough. There are pictures of me with a black bow tie in my pony tail—Father's touch. Mother wouldn't let me wear the handlebar mustache he gave me. She said it would make me cough. Ergo the recurring nightmare in which I'm in a play and can't find the costume. As I am walking out on stage, naked, I realize that I have never seen the script. Buzzy crouched behind the curtain and whispered lines to me, and to everyone else apparently, because the audience found us an entertaining twosome, although he was mostly out of sight. The Aho family laughed themselves beet-red. Mrs. Gravelhead prepared us for Jack Benny Junior High School. I still have a picture of her, cat-eye glasses and a brown, coifed hairdo called a bubble. She is wearing a black checkered dress and is standing in front of an enormous American flag.

Greenwood Street

started at the Johns Manville factory on Lake Michigan. Their parking
lot fed into and out of Greenwood Street so it filled up every morning
and afternoon with traffic. Don's father worked there making machine
parts. My father didn't work at the factory. He rode the train to
Chicago. Sometimes we went along, the rhythm of the train, green
windows, towns called: *North Chicago, Lake Forest, Highland Park,
Glencoe, Winnetka, Evanston, Skokie*. And my parents' friends didn't
work at the factory either. Waukegan was a bedroom to the city. We
didn't know the factory workers who drove past our house every morn-
ing and evening. They lived in the project on the other side of an
enormous field at the other end of Greenwood Street, where houses
were smaller, where kids drank more and got arrested sometimes, where
my boyfriend lived. No one I knew fell in love with a doctor's son. We
wanted working-class style, liked the boys with slick hair, tight jeans,
fast cars, slow smiles and warm arms, boys with rolling heads, fast hands
and bad grades. And they came over to the neighborhoods their fathers
drove through for the girls. The boy who gave me a bright silver going-
steady ring that I wrapped with white angora yarn to match my white
angora hat and sweater, lived in the project. And it wasn't that he had
failed a grade or that his car was fast, it was class, the way he talked,
double negatives, bad grammar, and that he never read a book he didn't
have to, that made my father dislike him, saying that he didn't dislike
him. It was just that he and I were different. I wrote him love letters
and poems. We passed notes and made out in his father's black Chevy
Impala, at the lake, next to the Johns Manville parking lot at the end
of Greenwood Street, every chance we got.

Sheridan Road

wound along the bluffs above the southern tip of Lake Michigan from Chicago to the southern border of Illinois and Wisconsin, was often mansion-lined and canopied by elm and maple trees. It was a busy street, unlike the quiet ones that ran through neighborhoods that spread out from the lake, or the congested cross streets that connected old parts of town to new developments of box houses and strip malls in a catastrophe of urban sprawl which criss-crosses area maps today like a iron grid leaving no green space between towns that, when I lived there, were separated by individual identities and long wooded bends in Sheridan Road. It went to Zion, curving along the way into a small group of luxury estates were Mary Golden's aunts lived. Mary lived in a mansion across the street from us on Greenwood Street, before we moved to Longview Street, and we were friends although our families seldom talked. When each child at school was asked what church they went to, Mary said that she was Jewish. The teachers invariably said, *"You're God's chosen people."* You could tell God had chosen Mary because she was very rich and beautiful and because she had a maid (Louise) and a chauffeur (Fred) who were black and lived in the basement. You could tell God had not chosen Louise and Fred. I wasn't sure I wanted to be chosen by God, which at my church meant you were born evil. Mary's family owned the best department store in town which seemed like a good thing to be chosen for—my understanding of history being somewhat limited. Her mother and father lounged in their pajamas having breakfast in bed weekend mornings while Mary and I played dolls in the next room. There were hundreds of dolls, and a thousand doll dresses which took several hours to put up. Mother and I went to Mary's store on sale day and bought scores of

Photo by James Dwight Safford

things from long tables where women elbowed each other digging for sweaters, skirts, scarves, purses, wallets and angora hats with matching gloves. Our money went with sales slips into vacuum tubes that shot change back to us. When Mary and I ran for the same student council office in high school, Ann's mother told me I would win because Mary was Jewish. When I got more votes, she was gracious, congratulating me as we sat by the window in her grandmother's pink satin sitting room. Later Mary dated an older boy whose Irish Grandmother used to take care of me, entertaining me by speaking in an Irish Brogue that was enchanting. I was in love with one of the boys who died in Vietnam, and having no idea that was going to happen, dove into the wild surge of the working class which meant I didn't see much of Mary even before my parents moved me out of town, away from Sheridan Road, and all the cross streets, cutting my high school career in two and saving me from enormous grief which they could see and to which I was entirely blind.

Flint

for Megan

My sister is an ancient piece of flint dropped ten
thousand years ago when a hunter fell in battle,
a spear head of stone chipped sharp, then aimed
at the heart of a great beast—
hit center
took life
and gave it back—
strong flint, a spear that outlasted the animal heart
and flew through time's fast air, a stone shaped like
a fish, a stone carved with the face of an owl.

You can still see the outline of the myth whose head
is a white bird emerging from stone. My sister is
sharp stone, rough scarred and ancient—
an arrow,
an emblem, an ancient piece
of flint.
Her name means *strong*.

Gold

How can a woman who lives in a circus run a business there,
saxophone honking into the telephone, rude child shouting
at clients?

How can she hope the newspaper will get printed, books
will get published on time, words will come out right side up?
Will the child ever learn how to tell time?

How can she know the child will learn to multiply
the modern way, not just how the Mayans did it?
How can a child make so many people angry?

How can she know the child whose mouth leaks foul language
endlessly will grow into a real human being, responsible, kind,
one who doesn't have to live in a cage?

How can she know the thread of her voice will endure
constant interruption, will learn to use the wild energy
of the circus, and not be drained by it?

How can she know the child honking
next to the telephone will one day pour gold from that—
or some other horn?

Doors

There were iris beds, a strawberry patch, a dog yard, a willow tree whose roots tangled into the septic tank, a dirt alley and a dozen neighbor kids out the back door of the house on Longview Street. Father stared out the window next to that back door every morning, drinking coffee and smoking. He stood there, and if I asked what he was doing he would say, *"Looking out the window."* Out the front door was a long porch, cool concrete, maple trees and pines, a lamp post, Longview Street, weeds, a cyclone fence, the golf course, then Sheridan Road. The cellar door opened horribly to dark steps, lined with mops, brooms, sponges, rags, cleaning brushes, vacuum attachments that followed children downstairs to a huge cellar with dark, high windows and a ringer washing machine which could swallow a child, shoelaces and all. Off to the side, under an eight-inch-thick concrete ceiling with a car parked on top of it, was a vault where we stashed supplies for nuclear attack or a tornado, whichever came first. The cellar door led to damp things, unfinished, underground things that made my heart beat fast, terror grabbing my throat and shoulder blades like claws that pulled me upstairs two steps at a time. The door to Grandmother's room was open. There was a closet door in her room where it smelled of skin oil and perfume, where nylon print dresses hung silent above grandmother shoes and purses. Grandmother was forbidden to go through the kitchen door when Mother was in there working. *"Can't she help?"* I asked, but Mother shushed me fast and Grandma pretended to be deaf.

The garage door led to a blue, four-door Ford Fairlane, that took us from Illinois to California, the car that got vapor lock in the mountains. The garage door also led to shelves and shelves of tools and gimcracks   Father used to fix things that were broken and vice versa. Once, to get a better view, Mother held the car door open while she backed out of the garage and left the car door jammed between the garage door elbow and the car. Once Father opened the large garage door, opened the car door, got in and backed the car in the garage into the car in the driveway. Later he said he'd always wanted to do that! Once Father slammed his finger in the car door, and once he slammed his finger in the garage door—index fingers on both hands, a matching set of vertical finger nails. One car door opened sideways, a lumpy brown Hudson Father bought for $50, the children's taxi, he called it, saying it wouldn't go fast enough for Mother to get a ticket, but she got one in the school zone in front of Greenwood Elementary School, the doors of which swelled with children of all descriptions, with multi-syllabic names from all over Europe, but when Grandmother asked me where my friends were

from, I'd say, *"America, Grandma!"* There were two bathroom doors, one in Grandmother's room; the other was the family bathroom in reference to which someone was always shouting, *"Shut the door."* There was a door to the front bedroom which was mine until Father built two rooms and another bathroom upstairs saying, *"Wouldn't it be nice for the girls to have a bathroom of their own, Anne?"* There was a door at the end of the hall between my room and the large bedroom where Mother and Father slept next to jewelry boxes full of expensive jewelry which Mother didn't like Father to spend money on, and costume jewelry she wore with color coordinated outfits. A plastic folding door petitioned off the nursery when my sister was a baby and there were sliding doors to Mother and Father's closets which were dark and full of costumes that were hilarious. There was no lock on the attic door behind which were murderers. I pushed a chest against the attic door at night. In the daytime it was safe. I smoked back there until Father suggested I would be less likely to burn the house down if I smoked in the bathroom with the fan running so no one would know. The door to

the upstairs bathroom was pink
and Formica around the two sinks
was pink and the towels were pink.
So were the walls. The door from
the dining room downstairs to the
living room was an open arch and
next to it was a brown arched tube
radio we gathered around at night
for radio dramas and world news in
the corner of the living room
furthest from the door to the front
hall closet, full of coats, where it
smelled like mothballs and where
Mother kept the fur coat she wore
when she dressed to go out the
front door with Father, who kept
his wallet, change, cigarettes and
matches on an antique table next
to the closet door, across from the
piano next to the fireplace over
which hung a large watercolor
painting of a polar bear standing
on an iceberg in the Arctic Ocean,
which Father said made him cold.
And there was the door to the
train Father disappeared into every
morning and stepped out of every
evening, a black steaming engine
pulling cars with green windows
behind which sat people reading
gigantic newspapers, a shrieking
trail of doors rolling and clattering
to Chicago and back, Chicago,
where doors were stacked on top of
doors in towers that turned streets
into canyons, where a child could
look up and not see the top, where
revolving glass doors spun, never
stopping, and an infinite tangle of
doors led to restaurants and depart-
ment stores, dentists and
bathrooms, elevators and stairwells
in patterns too complex for a
child's understanding and for that
reason—
exhilarating.

Longview Street

I could see Father from the front yard
and knew when he'd be home
by his long-legged gait that might
have been a limp except he was too
clever, and looked instead as if
he were going to change direction,
but his course was firm.

I could see past the driving range
which was directly across
the street from our house, past the
swimming pool at the top
of the hill where I spent most of my
time, past Grandmother
sunbathing in the front yard until
Mother caught her there.
It was easy to find my father from a
distance,
so I was seldom lost.

I could see over cyclone fences, yard to yard to yard to yard,
to swing, to junglegym, to sandbox. Hoards of kids played
long games of *Kick-the-Can* yelling,
"All yee! All yee In Come! Freedom!"
dashing for the goal in Bobby's front yard after supper
which was between six and seven on Longview Street
depending on where the fathers worked or how long
it took to have *"enough to drink."*

There were boys next door.
Bobby was invisible at school but we were friends
on Longview Street. Father said his brother was smart
and I should come inside when he bothered me.
Bobby's brother liked to wrestle me to the ground
in the side yard. Bobby told me girls and boys
were exactly the same except inside out.

Longview Street was one block long and ran alongside
Glenflora Country Club at the northern end of town
connecting Sheridan Road to North Avenue which went
all the way downtown to Genesse Street, which once
we could drive, was part of the *loop* we *scooped*
looking for boys.

Hangout was on the other side of the *loop*,
in the YMCA gym, upstairs from the pool where I learned
to swim. *Hangout* was a block away from the church
where Mother, Grandmother, Sister and I attended
three-generation potluck suppers that teenagers didn't *scoop*
on purpose in spite of the Young Methodist Christian Association
which we were encouraged to attend.

Hangout was wildly free, and every Friday night it was
the center of the world for several hundred high school kids,
though college boys sneaked in sometimes mistaking neighborhood
kids for fast girls, which we sometimes were.
Everybody danced—

the *jitterbug*, the *chicken*, the *jerk*, the *twist*, or we *slow danced*—
a hyper-ventilating, dizzy, teenage drape—stacks of 45 records
spinning 'till eleven which left time for a *fast* trip to the beach—
steaming up the windows, touching *there, but not there!* then back
to Longview Street before curfew, 11:45 or midnight.

From Longview Street to the *loop*, two miles.
From *Hangout* to the lake five minutes.
From the lake back to Longview Street—
thirty years.

A Book, or a Gate, More Like a Gate

I have been trying to remember the name of the boy who was riding a
touring car full of people from various segments of my life, mis-matched,
a roaming car that runs from the end of one dream to the middle of an-
other, and back, and forth. He got out in front of Dan's Hamburgers and
disappeared before I had time to ask him how he was. For months I've
been trying to remember his name. What I actually remember about the
boy was watching him *makeout* with Linda in the backseat—a two-year
breath-by-breath warm-up to ecstasy. It was a Polish name. I came in-
doors to find my shoes so I could feed the dogs, but reached up instead
for a book stacked flat on the top shelf of the bookcase next to my bed—
a book, more like a gate into a version of myself, a girl folded into the
spine of a two-page spread—the flute section in Otto Graham's High
School Concert Band, a girl in a surge of faces, faces I remember, perhaps
I saw them yesterday. Another boy, the one who died in Vietnam, left a
cryptic, scratched out note, *"Remember the argument!"* I find him sitting
cross-legged in the first row of the football team, scowling. Here, he is
bare-chested in a wrestling photograph—scowling. We went on a picnic
to Wisconsin with his whole family. His father had a toothache and
shouted at him. I said it was because of the pain, and he said, *"No way."*
His mother made potato salad and pickles and his sister chased two small

children around the backyard of a project house on a street with no trees. Someone wrote a note on the inside front cover, *"I hope you marry Don."* I was sixteen years old, wed in people's mind to a boy whose father yelled at him, a boy with dark, tanned skin, a handsome boy who quit school after his sophomore year, who joined the Marines, a boy who found arguments everywhere, who got roaring drunk with the one who rode the dream car to Congress Avenue, whose name I have been trying to remember. These boys in the book were trying to be leaders, to be popular and strong. They were dating girls from neighborhoods away from the projects, where streets were lined with trees. Outside the temperature is 105 degrees. It is July in Texas and I am forty-nine years old. I am playing ball with two dogs, a white coyote/shepherd and a calico ridgeback with Australian shepherd markings. The white dog is thirteen years old and falls down all the time. The other one is a puppy who has eaten one each of three sets of shoes. They have been waiting for me to come out for two hours. The boy's name was Smirtnick.

Heartland— a Eulogy

And why, after three decades, am I furious at a place itself, like any place, neutral. The boys, for instance— Larry, who walked home from a football game, three miles, with a broken shoulder—didn't he know it hurt? Or Chuck, the gentle eyed son of a man who worked at the factory and a woman from Puerto Rico. There were whip marks on his back, dozens of them. The other boys said, *"Don't ask."* Or Don, with whom I was in love most of the time, except he kept breaking up with me and coming back, and breaking up, and coming back. Dick was one of the intelligent boys. When he gave the right answer in class, teachers nodded. When I raised my hand they wrote notes to my mother saying, *"Tell Susan not to raise her hand so often."* Charles was an idiot, and made no bones about it. Everyone expected it of him. He was sleepy at school and invisible every place else. And Bob, a tall boy, long legged, wry sense of humor, he was a steady, gentle boy. There was nothing wrong with these boys. They were boys. They were doing what was expected of them, were the first wave of the Baby Boomers, children of men who had gone ashore on D-Day, storming over a line of dead bodies, a fly infested mangle of body parts as far as the eye could see, water lapping red brown sea foam. They were the sons of men who had flown B-52 fighter planes in Africa, who had dropped bombs on Dresden, or Hiroshima. They were the first born and final salvation of men who had opened the gates of Dachau and Auschwitz. There was nothing wrong with these boys. In fact, they had everything going for them, were American—sons of the victors. They lived in sturdy houses, with basements and wood paneling, on safe streets in the heartland of America. Their fathers developed Napalm, machine parts for every kind of weapon, built cars, sold tobacco, held the fabric of American society together, knit by knit, pulling tight ladders of success, covering their backsides. There was nothing wrong with these boys, the sons of survivors, with their little league baseball uniforms in the summer, ice hockey skates in winter, with their rolling eyes and fast hands. Their crude humor and distaste for school were normal. Everyone hated school, even the ones who liked it, hated school. Why did I set out at eighteen like a caged bird set free, and flying never look back, why did a girl from the Heartland spend her entire adult life unknitting the fabric, unraveling threads, finding rage, outrage, finding again and again the question—what was the matter with these boys? How could we have allowed our government to kill so many of them? Were there no wise women to warn, *"Look to your children, danger awaits them."* What happened to the Heartland that it could be so heartless, and not know it?

Photo by James Dwight Safford

Conscription

We were standing on Margo's deck
in Michigan, hadn't met since childhood.
He said,
*"Judy and I were talking about the sixties.
Free love, drugs, openness—it wasn't like that.
It was chaotic."*
"You went to Vietnam?"
"I went."

He was my cousin.
He was talking about the economy.
I was trying to remember why
I didn't know he was in Vietnam.
*"I've spent whole college educations
getting ready for vacations that cost thousands
of dollars themselves."* he said,
*"Now the economy is dead. Half the men
my age in Flint, Michigan are out of work."*

"I didn't know you went to Vietnam."
"I almost refused."
"People didn't know—"

*"By then we knew. I had to ask myself
if I loved my country enough to kill for it—
and then if I loved it enough to die for it—
for no reason.*

*"I carved my name beneath Grandfather's
on the back of the campaign trunk
he used in W.W.I.*

*"J. D. Safford
Joined May 12, 1918
J.D. Safford, Jr.
Conscripted August 16, 1968."*

Bottom photo self portrait by James Dwight Safford

Easy on the Brakes

After I left the Midwest I called a certain scrape of cirrus clouds a Midwestern sky, indicating dull and early darkness, the possibility of snow, indicating cold. In the Midwest there were marathons of snow, snow creatures that were part of the community, jagged ruts in the street, stiff like pie crust. We had long scraping tools for windows and it took half an hour to warm up the car. But snow didn't stop us; we slapped chains on car tires, or changed to snow tires with metal spikes in them for traction. Great yellow plows worked round-the-clock for months, clearing paths through slanting drifts, spreading salt and sand. Roads flew to surreal angles as cars slid in and out of lanes, across and through each other, piled up in ditches. Trucks jack-knifed. We packed extra clothing in the trunk for emergencies—and sand, shovels and a blanket or boards to put under the back tires to get out of being stuck. There were hours of things to try before you called the tow truck. You shoved the car into *"first, then reverse, first, reverse, just a little gas"*—never spin the tires. Along the Texas coast I watched a grown man sink a Winnebago into sand by flooring it. In snow you don't spin wheels, or use the breaks, gears slow you down. You steer—and pray or stay home until it blows over. People who give cars to teenagers in winter are insane. Give them a rich smelling, wax smooth toboggan or a sled. Or ice skates. We lived in skates, with rubber skate guards for the sidewalks or to walk across snow between ponds which were everywhere. We rode the bus in ice-skates, boots strung together, looped around our necks. It was cold. Breath steam rose up from our talk, our cheeks were blotched, and our toes took a long time to thaw out when we went indoors, which was intolerably hot and stifling to children who had been out in the snow. Snow was beautiful sometimes, blinding light exploding from the earth, dazzling ice turning trees into dancing white elves. You could make virgin footprints. More often it was slush, dirty, wet, horribly cold when it got into your boots or down your neck. Boys loved to stuff snow down a girl's collar. I remember knowing how to move in snow, and I remember the way ice could rip your feet out from under you. I remember amazing prat falls, wind you couldn't stand up in, waiting for the bus, bundled up every place except a six-inch gap between the top of my long socks and the hem of my skirt.

My knees would glow, beet red first—then blue. I remember driving
home from school through sloughs of gray slush after dark, being dazzled
by snow light the morning after a blizzard, landing cars in ditches, zig-zag
spinning down a hill, taking out a row of mail boxes, leaving every other
one standing on alternate sides of the street, landing sideways across the
entrance to a one lane bridge. I remember Father saying to go easy on
the brakes.

Locker Room

By the time I was in junior high our
schools were integrated, but I had no idea
where the black children came from
because I had never seen a black home.

Ivy
was in my gym class. Her locker was across
a narrow yellow bench from mine so we
knocked butts and elbows all the time.

Ivy
sang *"Poison Ivy"* at the top of her lungs in
the locker room and rolled deodorant on
the outside of her sweater because,
"I stink, I got cooties," she said.
"Now I don't stink no more."

Cheryl,
was quiet. She rolled her copper-colored
hair into a neat pageboy, like mine,
and we were friends—
at school.

I asked Mother if I could invite her home?
"Absolutely not," she said.
"Why not?" I didn't understand—

I didn't understand because the racism
woven into every fiber of culture
in the Heartland, was not discussed,
except as a problem *bigots in the South*
would be forced by the government
to solve.

Photos by James Dwight Safford

Main Street

In the Heartland
Main Street intersects
Center Street
downtown
right next to
Bogie's Restaurant
and the
Mobile Station.

If you keep going
on Main Street
there's a dead
end.

If you veer off
to the left
you can take
the
highway
out of town.

That's what I did.

Freeway

Railroad tracks and freeways, trailer trucks, freight trains,
commuters and tourists, gray light and the radio.
Sales people, bankers and lawyers, baseball players
rolling into Chicago, to commerce and glitz,
to culture, to theater and art—
to Wrigley Field, to Michigan Avenue—
every kind of person falling into the cadence,
falling at the great magnet—
from the suburbs, from the cornfields
from bedroom communities which themselves
created infrastructures and then abandoned
them when people from East Chicago moved upshore
in the last half of the twentieth century.

"That's East Chicago," I say to my son.

Traffic crawls past gigantic apartment blocks—
a tenement slumland, laundry hanging against yellow brick—
strung from window to window, collecting soot,
trading carbon monoxide for sweat,
vast weather beaten freeway lanes cracked, trashed out
pedestrian bridges at infrequent intervals.
Twelve lanes of traffic divide it from its slightly less horrific
self, violence blowing in the lake's harsh wind.

"It's a war zone." he says.
"No one would want to live here."

D.C. Cloud

lived in a maroon Nova parked on flat tires next to my son's school until
the City impounded his car, which was also his house. The macrobiotic
restaurant gave him large servings of food—sweet potatoes, beets, beans,
vinaigrette, ginger sauce, until they noticed him dumping their gifts in
the recycle bins at the end of the driveway. D.C. would rather have a
hamburger, but if they gave him a few dollars, he'd buy beer. *"D.C. is
nice,"* my son tells me. *"He used to be a runner and he trained for the
Olympics, but when he started drinking his family was ashamed of him so he
has to live here and they don't want to talk to him."* We are driving home, a
home with doors and windows, where people take care of each other,
particularly when they're sick. D.C. has moved out of the Nova, but he
hasn't left the area, lives alongside the river, holding on to the cracks in
urban America. We see him, tall stick-of-a-man, walking to and from the
dumpster in back of the convenience store where a colony of homeless
people meet mornings and afternoons. Yesterday, D.C. slept on a flat-
tened refrigerator box most of the day. His friends moved off to the side.
A steady stream of car and foot traffic pretended not to notice D.C.
living as if three trailer parks, eight restaurants, a school, two ball fields,
a community theater, the City Utility Works Maintenance Department,
the Fire Workers Union and four fast food joints were a camp ground for
him to roam, frail as a twig, dwindling to nothing, waiting to die, kind to
the children, dull to his own suffering and to hope.

Impact

1:45 PM
on the freeway,
at fault, a policeman
driving an unmarked car,
brakes locked,
swerved to the right, which I saw in time to brake, in time to move to
the exit lane, almost to the ramp at 38th Street, but not in time to avoid
impact which smashed my van, shut down the engine, sent me coasting
in slow motion down the exit ramp, across the frontage road, vacant,
silent like a dream. Twice I have walked out of firestorm accidents, the
car sailing out of control into oncoming traffic, twice the path has been
clear, twice I have ended up with nothing but these strange headaches
which make zig-zag lights vibrate, or stripes turn inside out. Mark Twain
said he used to swim the Mississippi River in the Spring, before it was
safe, when the currents were swift, and he'd get carried off, or under, and
someone would have to pull him out and inflate his lungs. Eventually,
shoremen called on his mother. *"Mrs. Clements,"* they said, *"why don't
you keep this boy out of the water?"* And she said, *"A child destined to hang is
safe in water."* Possibly, I'm safe in traffic. Perhaps there's a lesson, like the
first time. I was forced off the road by a woman who ran a stop sign. I
swerved to miss her, headed straight at a tree which I swerved to avoid,
short circuiting the car's forward momentum, flipping it twice, landing
sideways in a lane of oncoming traffic. My sister and I had enough time
to crawl out. I had enough time to notice there was blood all over her.
She had enough time to say it was my blood, before the car blew up, all
this during rush hour, in a double lane of traffic which was for some rea-
son, empty and silent, like a dream. I remember impact then too, how I
flinched for years if someone cut out in front of me. I remember saying
out loud, as the car rolled over, as strange a sensation as I have ever
known, that I wasn't going to die. I wondered afterwards if everyone
thinks that, and some are right, like I was, others—wrong. I remember
the driver who caused the first accident left the scene and lied about it in
court, opening the justice system for me like a carton of rotten milk. A
girl from the Heartland learns hard, if at all.

Mother Buddha

Mother Buddha waits for the blood to stop, joints stiffen and the points
of her smile turn down. She is depressed and the people in her family
hate her. She is hounded by men, or ignored, invisible in fact.
Old women fall in droves into great holes of uselessness. I can't go there.
The mother in me dies. I am the forgotten child, grown tall,
leaning into an age of power, an age when women don't have to take
care of anyone, an age to manipulate the threads of art, weaving,
weaving, singing. I sleep. Mother Buddha, fat with expectation, stops
expecting, blinks and rolls over. Am I a nun dreaming I am a butterfly,
or a butterfly dreaming I am a nun? I don't need men, am unlikely
to kneel down to abuse. It is time to leave. How to leave the family?
It ought to be possible to do it without their even noticing.
The time of the fat Mother Buddha is past. Is it time to turn cold,
harsh and cynical? Or to be an evangelist, wear white robes and preach
like Marjorie Kemp, in the twelfth century, who birthed thirteen
children, sued for divorce, married god—then spiraled into holy vision?
Who better to appreciate holiness? How to call down the mother?
Held too long it is destructive as anything I can think of.

Photo by James Dwight Safford

The Second Half of the Life of the Woman

begins in a cloud of change, begins with feeling powerless and unwanted, begins with children screeching *"Leave me alone!"* and men going elsewhere for nourishment, begins with her own parents dying, begins with body creaks and misshapen form. She has been the most beautiful girl at the dance, or not. She has been student and wife, a young artist, passionately attacking the great hoax of adulthood. She has been the child, waiting off stage, wondering if anyone will show her the script. She has watched children dying in the cancer ward, and wept and seen war after war after war after war parade across the face of the century. She could die now, but she won't, is too ornery. Alone in spite of the circle of hunger around her, power burns from a belly hollowed out, she moves past the lover she met head on and past the lover she avoided, she hovers wondering what to do next. She has made choices, has regrets. She has caused pain when she intended to heal, and found health in wild mountain clouds above knowing. She dreams her father has come back to life and she dances around him. She is a woman, has been motivated by love her entire life. Now she looks for ambition, for the seeds of it. Necessity drove her into the marketplace, she was alien there, a zebra in a traffic jam, discordant, her songs spill into hearts there for sale. It's a mystery, the joke that is true, the passion beneath the passion, the complicated one, that tears truth out, chews it up, spits it out, sells it, raucous melodies, twinkling eyes, an old love song. She was serenaded and closed the porch windows, went downstairs to make supper. But she got there too late, the song was engraved in her soul. After one hearing, it stuck and fell into the stew. All of her children were artists. These things happened in the first half of the life of the woman. What will she create from their ambiance, where will she go to revel in white hair and old friends? Out, out, further out into the marketplace. Out to the world, woman leaping out of the circle of love, past the fire of the hearth, out to Planet Earth with an agenda, *"the look of a woman who exists in the world to change the world."* (Muriel Rukeyser) What will it be like, this market that turns into a mother?

They Were A Violent People

How things are now?
We unravel knots that lured them into conflict.
We had to. The knots were snake pits.
We learned to co-exist with snakes.
We learned to seek defeat as well as victory.
We honor both.
Today we each exist on both sides of the wall.
We do not have guns or bombs or mind control.
We have unknit the military complex in our hearts
and in our institutions.
We do not **invade** each other.

Healers move gently through the river of the spirit.
We embrace light at the edge of the void by diving
free form into it.
We luxuriate in space and spirit freely entered.
How can I tell you of the exhilaration that blows
across a life when the veil of violence lifts.
We go unmasked into the future.
Fear and joy sound together in our mating call,
it resonates as mind and body integrate.

No one is correct.
The last right person died in 2027 clutching a concrete
tablet etched into his forehead.
We mourn him. We mourn his position.
It is part of our *Celebration of Freedom.*
Our *Celebration of Freedom* is a gift we offer
to the Universe in exchange for existence.
It has nothing to do with Nationalism or Religion.
They are antique.

Now, power and magic belong to the individual.
We roam the universe at will with the same skill
we aim at our own hearts.
Struggle for balance is the air we breathe.
We are at peace.
It happened when they conceived of it.

Human nature changed.
Here is a song we sing during the
Celebration of Freedom.
It has been sung so long no one
can remember where it came from.

*"Mourn for the preacher
if you want to,
mourn for the soldier
if you can.*

*But do not cry for me.
I have gone to live
in the next eon,
I've moved to the next age.*

*Parents give their children
to the winds of change,
people give their labor
for the grain of peace."*

Photo by James Dwight Safford

Our Lady of Guadalupe

December 12 at 3 o'clock in the morning, the people of Guadalupe parish celebrate her birthday—a thousand rose petals, velvet cool scent against night air. An Aztec drum vibrates. *The goddess does not fade.* Roses, Roses— On the altar, in the aisle, in people's arms, singing. Roses, in the cold dead of winter. *Guadalupe came before Juan Diego time after time and said, "Tell the bishop to build me a shrine here."* On the first Saturday in September, a pig farmer, some men who work in a cement factory, some men from the parish, and a young girl, whose great-grandparents gave land to the parish to build Guadalupe church, whose name the bright eyed nuns from Ireland do not recognize, who has lived all her life in an ancient, small house out back of the church, who is Guadalupe—gather. *Her image fell into the cloth of Juan Diego's cape. Once a year villagers crawl on their knees from the mountains down to the shrine in the city to see the cloth.* They rehearse a play five hundred years old, a medieval pageant play that came from Spain, except that the characters are Indian. *Her image falls into the tangle of our lives. Bring candles to celebrate her birthday, candles and roses.* They rehearse outdoors in the backyard of the church. They perform all over San Antonio, in rain and snow, weekends and at night, always outdoors, in all kinds of weather, they play out the pageant. Their voices are mumbled. Now for the first time in four hundred years the play has been printed. An actor from the art center offers to help them with their blocking. The loudest voice is Lucifer—Victor Elizondo plays Lucifer. He once led a sacred dance troupe. His magic is astounding, he can even be invisible. Father Salazar says the players practiced in the backyard of the church for two years before he realized they existed. *Los Pastores* in New Mexico is directed by Victor Elizondo's cousin. The design on his cape is the head of a free dragon. He has given that cape to his son and is making a new one. *Juan Diego said the bishop would pay no attention to him, said he was not important enough to speak to a bishop.* Roses and candles, candlelight and the barrio, a cold winter morning, 3 a.m. In Mexico City at the shrine of Guadalupe, the image of Juan Diego is cast across the iris of the eye of the goddess shrouded in his cape. *Some say the cloth where her image still holds is a contract between Indigenous and European peoples.* Father Salazar on a white horse, draped with roses, leads the procession, singing to the shrine of an Aztec Saint, alive as a rose, pulling nutrients still from civilizations entwined like plants and the earth.

Ricardo

Ricardo is standing in front of my desk. Tears are streaming
down his face but he isn't crying. He is shouting at me.
"Everything is narrow."
I am watching a double scar that runs from the center
of his forehead to his chin.
"I read Jonathan Edwards and Benjamin Franklin!
I tell you what I think and you say it is wrong.
What I think isn't wrong."

He is telling me that he didn't speak English until
he was fourteen years old. He is telling me that he was riding
the bus and reading Jonathan Edwards—
"That guy was crazy."
I tell him that what he thinks about Jonathan Edwards is right,
but his paper is in the wrong form. He is telling me form
doesn't matter.

Ricardo is six feet tall and built like a tank.
He is apologizing for yelling at me.
He doesn't need to apologize for anything. I like Ricardo.
He is telling me he is frustrated.
"College isn't for people like me."

I tell him I will show him how to fix his paper but
he isn't listening. He is telling me that his parents
were killed when he was three years old.
When I look at him I see tears pouring out—
He is saying that he should go back to fixing cars.

Ricardo says he wanted to be a teacher to help Mexican
children, so they wouldn't have to grow up on the street
like he did. His arms and chest are scarred. There are scars
on his thighs, large marks, as if he'd been thrown
through plate glass. He tells me he's been left twice
for dead.

He says he quit school in the sixth grade. I say that's what
happens to the smart ones. They can't stand it.
He stops raging for a second.
"That's right," he tells me. *"That's what happens."*

I tell Ricardo I am honored that he chose to talk to me.
He tells me he doesn't know why he is crying.
"I'm a tough guy."
"You're covered with scars. That's why you're crying.
I'm crying too."

A year later I see Ricardo at a fish market on the Texas Coast.
He tells me the prices are too high and where to get a better deal.
He introduces me to his girlfriend as the lady who failed him
in English. I say,
"That's not fair, you never came back to class."

Ricardo is laughing at me.
I say, *"Go back to school."*
But the schools are wrong.

Photo by James Dwight Safford

Luck

I took the child to the lake.
He was fishing but he wasn't patient,
got up and left the fishing pole
lying on the ground too close to the water.

He had a fish but he wasn't watching
until too late, until he saw his rig
disappear into the water, gone.

"It took my pole!" he could hardly believe it.
"The fish took my whole pole!"

"Cast in with your pole!" he shouted to his brother.
"Don't bug me man, I'm fishing."

We cast out a grappling hook.

"It came back up!" he said.
*"It came right back up! The whole thing—
hook, line, reel, pole and a huge catfish!"*

The boy was young. His luck had not run out.

Photo by James Dwight Safford

Monique

Moon-eyed girl with silk hair and black lips
dressed like a prostitute, breaking rules,
herself broken by alcohol, by smoke, by rape,
writing hot checks.

Monique, at ten—
following her mother everywhere
doing the laundry, taking care of the younger
children, gracing the house with her light.

Monique, at twelve—
asking her mother at the funeral,
*"Why are you saying all those good things
about Grandmother? She was a bitch."*

Monique, at fifteen—
living on the street, fighting with her father
trashing out her life with smoke, with crack, alcohol.

The telephone answering machine says—
"Pay, or die."
Monique saying she has been invited to be a call girl
in Houston.
"I won't have to do anything. It's just lonely old men."

Monique, at sixteen—
saying, *"I just want to float away."*

Green Ice Cream

In the laundromat a girl—
blonde stringy hair, four years old, sits high up
on a bench. She is eating green ice cream.

Green ice cream covered with a thin layer of dark black
chocolate drips, streaks her face with fluorescent
creme de menthe green, green streaks her shirt.

Smudges of chocolate stick to her knuckles,
then her cheeks. It looks like she has been shattered
and green fluorescence is oozing out of cracks in her face.

She is holding a puppy, limp from hours of childlove,
"Look, it can curl up into a ball!" she says, smushing it up.
"Look at my puppy!"

A man is doing laundry.
"O dear, she dropped her ice cream," he mutters
but he doesn't wipe up the green ice cream.

He doesn't clean off her face or shirt or knuckles
or talk to her or help her take care of the puppy
which is half dead.

Green ice cream melts into a slick plastic mass
on the floor near the door at the laundromat.
Neglect.

Chance

"Do you think I have a chance?"

"You have a chance."

He tells the other children at the hospital,
"I'm going to get out!"
and they all cheer.

"But what about my mom and dad?
They will say no."

"I know it."

"But they don't matter, do they?"

"I don't know."

"The court can tell them to leave me alone, can't they?"

"Yes it can."

"Can I come live with you?
My mom and dad don't want me any more."

Borazine

Imagine you have been abandoned
by your parents, separated by Mother State
from your twin, adopted by people who
abandoned you in a lock up mental ward—

Imagine, in spite of this
you are not crazy—
or even sick, just angry and scared.
Imagine that you can't sit still.

"They gave me borazine."

"What happened?"

"I didn't want to, but I went to sleep."

Later,
when they began to let him leave the hospital,
he'd sometimes get angry.

And he would shout—

"Can't you just give me a shot?"

Photo by James Dwight Safford

Bent Machete

"You say you want to call your brother," the group leader says at breakfast, *"but you don't want to call your brother. I don't see you helping clear the table—"* The table has already been cleared. The group leader is grasping at straws, as if someone said, *"Find something to criticize."* One girl puts her head down on the table. The others glaze over. They are used to it, adults are going to invent things to get on their case about. It is a therapeutic technique. Whatever the child wants, they can't have because they have done something wrong, or need to do something they haven't done. Rewards come at random after everything has been taken away by adults who have this power because they are adults. And the children have always done something wrong. You can count on it, children screw up all the time, it's practically the definition of childhood. But these children screwed up big time, were born to the wrong parents, look at the case histories, or at Frankie's skull, the rude scar shaped like a bent machete. Children, moths to light, never smile, justice always leveled by authority that is alternately kind and cruel, from God down to the cafeteria table where the group leader drones on, *"No, I don't believe you will be calling your brother today."*

Photo by James Dwight Safford

Bird Girl

Hot October sunlight. The program leader is whittling. All morning he has been sitting in the shade, whittling, visiting with people who drive up in vans, double-cab pick-up trucks, staff. He is working with six girls who are sitting in a circle at the center of which is a stone. Hot sunlight bakes them to submission, just outside the rim of his shade tree. With a gold knife he is carving a walking stick which he has propped between his knees. Slowly, with the hands of an artist, he pulls a snake head from the wood, a long stick of wood which he holds between his knees. The girls may not speak or look up, their heads are bent down, to shade eyes from sunlight. Possibly they have been insubordinate to their counselor, or cruel, or worse. Today they will sit all day in a circle. The stone at the center of the circle is their *group leader*. At noon the girls are excused from circle to go to lunch. On the way out of the cafeteria one flails, kicks a foot out, waves her arms, bird like, bird child, trying possibly to fly away. Rumor has it both her parents committed suicide, that she is troubled, keeps trying to fly, flailing. Flailing air brushes against the Program Leader's ankle, not a kick to the shins, just a brush of air, wing space rippling October sunlight, heat waves. He tackles her. Fast, fast, so that instantly the girl is pinned down, flat on her back, a man on top of her, wrists grasped, a knee holding her pelvis fast against the grass. First she was sitting in the circle, a stone at the center, then the cafeteria, now she is flat on her back, the bird child whose touch is as rough as a twig snapping, a leaf falling. The wood carver is breathing on her face. *"No arms or feet striking at me. Do you understand?"* Ninety-eight degrees, high noon sunlight. Her eyes are closed, throat sounds, *"Daddy no, Daddy no."*

Photo by James Dwight Safford

Nisaba

Summarian Scribe,
circa, 2700-2300 BC
Menil Museum, Houston

Woman standing,   knees bent,
arms folded   over stomach—
reeling   head tilted back
to sky   in anguish,
arms folded   across womb,
cradle   of civilization.
Terra cotta   woman—
standing   at the dawn
of history,   scribe,
shreiking at   *Sky,*
reeling.   3687 years later,
give or take   a few centuries,
I have come   out from
woman/anguish   to find you,
Nisaba,   ancient one:
Send me power,   to transform
the emperor   whose passion
is control;   send me power
to live fully,   love completely,
with wisdom   and grace;
send me power,   *Fire*
and endurance;   send me power
to be whole,   not divided.

Let me ride   the lion
and enjoy   and not be food;
send me power   and a thread
to follow;   help me
find a way   through the maze
of woman/soul;   lead me back
to the deep   healing
of language,   the power

of symbol.   Nisaba,
woman standing   at the dawn
of history,   translucent—
take me back   there
to the first   *Word;*
teach me well   that I may sing
again your song,   the one
that can transform   the blow.

Big Nurse

Yesterday Big Nurse was a man, long dick hanging
under bloated stomach, hard in a room full of children.
She fumbles for words. He stalks or traps anyone
in his path. There are children in his care.
He is a woman today, swirling in the kitchen, selling
t-bone steaks to oil field workers hired to guard
children they are too ignorant to teach.
He's a gentleman, a snake, a cow with as many
teats as there are children.
Everyone knows he is in charge.

Everyone is stone, inside and out, except the ones who fight
and they end up with broken legs or heels (saying
"I fell off the swing.") or souls.
Yesterday I saw Big Nurse at the Therapy Ranch
where they neither ranch nor provide therapy
but the state gives them seventy-two thousand dollars
per child, per year and Big Nurse is there in person
and she/he calls the shots.

Photo by James Dwight Safford

School at the Boy's Ranch

"It don't make no difference." said the teacher.
"Take a seat." One boy says he doesn't understand
how to do his work. *"Yes you do,"* she says,
"Yes you do know how to do it."
There is an ancient computer in the class.
No one is using it. In the entry way to the school,
is a gleaming row of color computers. No one
is using them. Uphill is a new swimming pool.
No one is using it.
One child does three spelling papers.
"You done all your spelling for the week.
What you gonna do tomorrow? "
"He's pretty good," she tells me
"If you can get him to work."
The child has twice her IQ.
"It don't matter." the child says.
I say *"You mean it doesn't matter."*
He tells the teacher, *"She wants me to speak correctly."*
"After you listen to them speak," she says,
"you get so you don't use the language right yourself.
It is the least of our problems."
Would she teach the children that 4 + 7 = 8?
Or to stand behind a mule and comb its tail?
Is she teaching the children about safe sex,
or how to survive child abuse?
How to type? Or write an essay? Or a story?
Can anyone tell me the capital of Cuba?
Or who is the governor of Texas?
Ignorance is ignorance and it starts with the words
running through your head and out your mouth.
Which is not to say the child's day was unsuccessful.
He didn't walk out in disgust.

Gladiators

They are gladiators, tagging the neighborhood with cans
of spray paint, flashing colors, spilling violent decibels
of sound from boom boxes, beepers hooked on to their belts,
heads full of spinning blades, flashes of light spinning
like spectrum circus balls, blood pours out of their eyes
and knee caps, hormones and crack splash in their brains.
They are gladiators, violent family circles inside a violent culture.
They walk with death, fall into to jail where
there's a chance they won't die tomorrow.

One morning in Texas I visited a second grade classroom—
A paid professional was administering standardized tests
in English to Spanish speaking children. I asked
what the tests were for. They seemed a waste of time.
They were for placement—
Educators wondering why children take to the streets.

But there are thousands of reasons children die inside—
Violent parents, dead parents, unavailable parents, poverty.
Now they're gladiators, three deep, dressed to kill, tattoos,
gimmie caps turned backwards. The one in the center
is eating an ice cream cone. He's bad.
Even eating a dairy swirl from the park concession stand,
he's bad. He is a gladiator, a veteran of blood theater.
One of the young boys is complaining. He's lost his belt.
"My pants fall down, man. My pants are falling down."
A child tags along eating cotton candy.

The boys I went to high school with ended up in Vietman.
These boys hit the street.
What does America have against it's children?

Bad

He beat up a friend
when he was eight,
spent two years
locked up in a juvenile
facility.

He came home
hung out
robbed stores
hung out.

He and a friend
stole a car
with a man in it,
a red car.

They smashed the car,
killed the man,
called their friends
on the car phone
and the police found them.

The young boy
fifteen—
hands cover face,
eyes roll back—

He is everyone's son.
The man he killed is your father.

Old Grandmother's Dream

I am alone, white hair caught in a hard wind.
I have reached the top of the mountain.

Tentacles of earth hold me here, exhilarated
after this climb that takes days.

I have come for a vision.
My head fills with discordant images.

I scratch at my eyes, shake my head, lean to earth
and vomit.

As far as I can see Earth is a tangled mass
of ugliness. There are no forests.

Taught cords stretch between trees that have been
stripped—roads are wide, rivers are dry.

The water is putrid, there are no wild animals.
Gigantic snarls of humanity choke the land.

It is the roar that makes me vomit.
War ships fly across cloud faces. People are brawling.

Sun shafts are violent and harsh—
unclean colors at twilight and at dawn.

Wind is a hot harsh scream that never stops.

Photo by James Dwight Safford

Mother Failure

It feels like I am a ship plowing through an ocean of
exhaustion. It feels like I am constantly teaching someone
not to be violent or aggressive.

It feels like I am being drained of life fluid by people who
are on fire. It feels like I am hanging on by woman/energy
alone.

It feels like I am not here in my body at all, my power is
absorbed by boys who are fighting. Why do I think I can change
them? Women for centuries have failed.

Photo by James Dwight Safford

Enheduanna Wrote on Stone

"Born ca. 2300 B.C., Enheduanna was a moon priestess, daughter of King Sargon of Agade who reigned over the world's first empire, extending from the Mediterranean to Persia. Enheduanna is the first writer, male or female, in history whose name and work have been preserved. Her personal history survives in highly political poems. We have a stone disk which contains a detailed likeness of the high priestess, revealing her particular features and dress, flanked by three of her retainers. The poetry we have has been preserved on cuneiform tablets. Quotations that follow are taken from adaptations by Aliki and Willis Barnstone of "*The Exaltation of Inanna*," Yale Univ. Press, 1968 by William W. Hallo and J.J. A. Van Dijk."

Enheduanna wrote on stone.
The first poet in recorded history
was a woman who wrote political poetry,
was a woman who gathered symbols,
mysterious and strange for us to see,
cut stone glyphs in order to catch thought—
to converse with holy ones.

How dull and heavy the medium,
sculpture to chase fleet passages
of mind, heartbeat,
cut stone words to throw at the goddess:

"Like a dragon you have filled the land with venom.
Like thunder when you roar over the earth,
trees and plants fall before you.
You are a flood descending from a mountain,
O primary one,
Moon Goddess Inanna of heaven and earth!
Your fire blows about and drops on our nation.

"Lady mounted on a beast,
An gives you qualities, holy commands,
and you decide.
You are in all our great rites.
Who can understand you?"

Enheduanna wrote on stone,
questions about divinity and human suffering,

questions about the vibrant green of Spring,
the black green of thunder, the violent green
of torrent, mountain emptying into ocean,
wars so violent even plants tremble.

"Storms lend you winds, destroyer of the lands
For you the rivers rise high with blood
and the people have nothing to drink.
The army of the mountain goes to you captive
of its own accord."

Your stone words fall out of history,
pour and tumble, rough and fierce
into my life.

It has always been so.
I have been singing this song
for so long my tongue grows thick,
numb, cold and sullen,
snake hair, stone face,
over and over,
since there were words we have used
them to unmask savage gods.

"You have lifted your foot and left
their barn of fertility.
The women of the city no longer speak of love
with their husbands.
At night they do not make love.
They are no longer naked before them,
revealing intimate treasures."

Words are fast now, fast words:
duality: man versus woman, good versus evil—
ownership: of people, property, boundaries, nationalism—
seeds of evil:
Conquest kills passion,
passion is the fire of life, holy flame.
Words: Deny the violent gods.

Words: Leap through the fire of your soul.
Words: Live, live!

Words are fast now, fly from river to sky,
continent to ocean, parent to child,
page to heart. In an instant,
the entire world can change its mind, everything is possible
planets converge, populations emerge, change, revolt
but it doesn't do any good.

We worship violent gods.
Enheduanna wrote on stone.
That is what she said.
She said we worship violent gods.

House of the Mother,
Gone.

In eighteen hundred it was an old wooden farmhouse
on Elk mountain, dark wood floors, a thin staircase
to wing dormers, brilliant with light, eccentric angled ceilings.
Downstairs—a huge fieldstone fireplace, Grandfather's brown
leather chair. Outside—a fieldstone front porch with rockers,
hydrangeas were tall as the banister, yellow roses.

It was a country estate, not a working farm.
Great grandfather was the minister of the church
across the meadow, on the other side of the graveyard,
where half the markers say *"Cure."*

The wagon wheels at the front gate came from the other side
of the family, the blacksmith who made wagons.

In 1950 the farm house was museum clean—
polished oak floors, a dark wooden staircase.
Stones on the front porch were swept fresh, dew cool.
The front gate was working and the side meadow sloped
down to the cabin I was born in and then to the creek.

In 1950 light streamed into the farmhouse through lace
curtains and the fireplace wall was lined with books.
There were violins and a piano, music stands and an organ
in the parlor which was a combination music and dining room.

Today I walked through the house my grandmother
inherited from her grandparents, the farmhouse grandfather—
against her wishes—sold to a farmer who breeds cows.

There is a swimming pool full of algae in the meadow
and most of Elk mountain has been cleared to grow hay.
A farmer, standing up to his ankle in black mud,
is unloading Black Angus bulls from a semitruck trailer.
His wife says my Grandfather gave them the farm
even though they couldn't make a down payment.

Grandmother's roses are gone, no hydrangeas.
The old wagon wheels are there but the front gate
is missing. A young bull prances across the side yard.
Orange shag carpet hides dark wooden floor boards
and the ceiling has been lowered with acoustical tile.
The fireplace is lined with carnival stuffed animals.
Dark curtains keep light from the house.

Grandmother's museum is a showcase for cupie dolls,
county fair things—papiér mâche parrots in brass rings,
Ferris wheels spinning above fake lakes painted on black velvet.
The staircase is hidden by red velvet curtains and the upstairs
bathroom is iridescent lavender—plastic curtains to match.

Life at the farm is less pristine than it was when
Grandmother polished old wood and played the violin
until thick and cool morning mountain mist lifted
from the petals of her grandmother's sunlight white rose.

Rafters

In the rafters, like a skeleton or a shadow—
In the rafters is a message—
Go back, go back to the beginning
of the family, to the soul torn apart—

Outside, a child is hunkered deep and laughing
in a patch of wild flowers, beside stone steps—
gone forever.

Go back to the past, to the language of the attic
stuffed with cobwebs, remodeled and rebuilt.
Go back, dust, dust, ceiling beams and rafters.

Go back to the skeleton, primal, elemental,
to the skeleton of the family just before humanity
outgrew the planet like the great monsters
that preceded us.

Somewhere—
in the rafters is a message we must take with us
as we leap out to the stars.

Do Not Forget in Peace Times

Jean Saint De Crevecoeur

Do not forget in peace times to teach the children
about violence, how it swirls out of the center of everyone,
how each must own their own quotient of it,
must order the chaos of it in their private soul.
Do not forget in peace times to teach the children, that
war seeds war, comes from unhealed fights whose blood raw
wounds callous over, hard and dull, doctrinaire—
like smooth silver film, a celluloid tablet of the world.
Do not forget in peace times to teach the children
how the wounded ones project their pain onto the world
at Auschwitz, or Salem, finding witches or Jews, or saints
or Iranians, or Africans, or anyone, maybe you.
Do not forget in peace times to teach the children
each act of violence seeds the next.

Photo by James Dwight Safford

128

Mother's Favorite Song

The song
that breaks through
is a soft one—
long
or eternal,
children laughing
singing
trilling their tongues,
syllables
and cadence,
sometimes shrill,
sometimes with gusto
or mellow—
water flowing
over creek stones
in a child's
soul—
thoughtless.

Photo by James Dwight Safford

About the Author

Susan Bright is author of fourteen books of poetry, three of which have been recipients of Austin Book Awards. She is the publisher of Plain View Press, which for the twenty years between 1975 and 1995 has published ninety-three books. Her work as a poet, publisher, activist and educator has taken her all over the country. In Texas she has received a proclamation from the Senate honoring her literary and community work and in Austin she received the Woman of the Year Award in 1990 from the Women's Political Caucus *"in recognition of outstanding leadership and initiative in helping to improve the quality of life for women and their families in Austin and Travis County."*

She works in a home studio near Austin's Barton Springs where she is a year around lap swimmer. She was the founding director of Texas Circuit, a literary organization serving Central Texas and is a founding board member of Parkside Community School, a non-profit Montessori-based community school. She is editor of *"Women's Way,"* a feminist newspaper and coordinator of the Women's Way Festival which has been held in Austin to celebrate Women's History Month every year since 1986.

House of the Mother is published in a first edition of 2000 the first 400 of which are signed and numbered.

This was the farm house in Deposit, New York where Maude Smith Safford grew up, and where she returned shortly before she died. She is standing at the end of the sidewalk.